W9-BYT-423

THE RECRUITING OFFICER

George Farquhar

The Royal Court Writers Series
published by Methuen
in association with the Royal Court Theatre

ROYAL COURT WRITERS SERIES

First published as a paperback original in 1988 by Methuen Drama
Michelin House, 81 Fulham Road, London SW3 6RB

Copyright in the commentary and format © Methuen Drama 1988
Copyright in the basic text © Ernest Benn Limited 1977

British Library Cataloguing in Publication Data
Farquhar, George, *1678-1707*
The recruiting officer.———(Royal
Court writers series).
I. Title II. Series
822'.4

ISBN 0-413-19630-5

Printed in Great Britain by Expression Printers Ltd, London N7 9DP

CAUTION
This book is sold subject to the condition that it shall not, by way of trade or otherwise be lent, resold, hired out, or otherwise circulated without the publisher's prior consent in any form of binding or cover other than that in which it is published and without a similar condition including this condition being imposed on the subsequent purchaser.

The front cover shows the 1774 election in the Square at Shrewsbury.
The picture is reproduced by courtesy of Rowley's House Museum, Shrewsbury.

COMING NEXT

IN THE MAIN HOUSE 730 1745

From 1st September
OUR COUNTRY'S GOOD

by Timberlake Wertenbaker
based on Thomas Keneally's novel *The Playmaker.*
Directed by Max Stafford-Clark

The Recruiting Officer company will also be seen in Timberlake Wertenbaker's new play. Set in the Convict colony perched on the rim of Australia in 1789, a young marine lieutenant directs a group of convicts through the rehearsals and production of *The Recruiting Officer*. Rehearsals are threatened — it's possible that the leading lady may be hanged, the colony's priest fears the production will be an incitement to immorality and the director has bad dreams.

Sundays 9, 16, 23, 30 October at 8.00pm

OCTOBER DAYS

DAGMAR KRAUSE

sings works by HANNS EISLER

Dagmar Krause is the finest contemporary interpreter of the German song tradition. Her latest work, devoted to the songs of Hanns Eisler, will be unveiled at the OCTOBER DAYS series of concerts.

IN THE THEATRE UPSTAIRS 730 2554

From 7 July
DOWNFALL

by Gregory Motton
Directed by Lindsay Posner

There is murder, longing and revolution in the City as the searchlights cut through the dark, dark night: a brilliant array of characters breaks from the shadows.

Gregory Motton's daring new play is a Royal Court commission and follows *Ambulance* seen UPSTAIRS in 1987.

"Beneath the jokes and punkish swagger it is a young voice of urban displacement and unlocated grief." Michael Ratcliffe, THE OBSERVER.

From 18 October
FOCO NOVO THEATRE COMPANY

present a remarkable new play

CONSEQUENCES

The future unfolded by:

Howard Brenton, Nell Dunn, Tunde Ikoli, Trevor Griffiths, Joshua Sobol, Tom Stoppard, Nigel Williams, Snoo Wilson and Olwen Wymark.

Directed by Roland Rees

Foco Novo, who for sixteen years have pioneered new theatre writing, have commissioned nine of Britain's top playwrights to work together and write an extraordinary new play.

Based on a fantastic dramatic game, CONSEQUENCES is a kaleidoscopic feast of farce, fantasy and vision which takes a humorous but searching look into the twenty-first century.

THE NEW PATRONAGE SCHEME AT THE ROYAL COURT

For the last three years the Royal Court has had to supplement its box office earnings and government grants with fund-raising from private business sources. While we have been relatively successful in meeting our fundraising targets and recent years have seen better and better earnings from the box office, the future looks as difficult as ever, in spite of the Arts Minister's announcement of a three-year increase in the Arts Council's grant-in-aid.
Increasingly, therefore, the Royal Court needs a body of regular support in its fundraising drive and so we are introducing our New Patronage Scheme. For many years now Members of the Royal Court Theatre Society have received special notice of new productions, but why not consider contributing £35 (or £50 joint membership) and become a **Friend of the Royal Court** — or approach your company or business to become an **Associate** or a **Patron**, thereby involving yourself directly in maintaining the high standard and unique quality of Royal Court productions — while enjoying complimentary tickets to the shows themselves?

1 MEMBERSHIP SCHEME

For £10 you will receive details of all forthcoming events via the Royal Court *Member's Letter*, and be entitled to purchase any available seat for £3 during previews (maximum of two per Member).

2 FRIENDS OF THE ROYAL COURT

For £35 (or £50 joint membership) you will be entitled to one (or two) complimentary preview ticket(s) for performances on the Main Stage and one (or two) exchange vouchers for productions in the Theatre Upstairs. You will automatically be on our mailing list and be invited to all lectures and special events.

3 ASSOCIATES OF THE ROYAL COURT

For £350 you will be entitled to four top priority tickets (previews or press nights) to all Main House productions, two tickets to all plays in the Theatre Upstairs and priority block ticket-booking availability. If desired, you can appear in the Royal Court programme.

4 INDIVIDUAL PATRONS

For £1,000 you can make a 'personal appearance' on a plaque in the Royal Court lobby, and appear in our programme. In addition, you will be entitled to six free tickets for shows in the Main House or the Theatre Upstairs.

When you have chosen from the four categories, please make your cheque/P.O. payable to the *Royal Court Theatre Society* and send to: *Max Stafford-Clark, Artistic Director, Royal Court Theatre, Sloane Square, London SW1*. Alternatively, if you wish to covenant for four years or more by filling in the form which you will find in the theatre foyer, we — as a registered charity — can claim back the tax you have already paid, thereby increasing the value of your donation.

PATRONS

Henny Gestetner, Tracey Ullman, Caryl Churchill

ASSOCIATES

Richard Barran, Davido Capelli, Michael Codron, Elizabeth Garvie, Patricia Marmont, Jonathan Miller, David Mirvish, Greville Poke, Richard Wilson, Sir Dermot de Trafford.

FRIENDS

John Arthur, Jim Broadbent, Guy Chapman, Angela Coles, C. Collingwood, Jeremy Conway, Lou Coulson, Alan David, Mrs. Der Pao Graham, Ann Diamond, R. H. & B. H. Dowler, Adrian Charles Dunbar, Jan Evans, Trevor Eve, Kenneth Ewing, Kate Feast, Gilly Fraser, David Gant, Kerry Gardner, Anne Garwood, Jonathan Gems, Sharon Hamper, Jocelyn Herbert, Derek Hornby, Dusty Hughes, Kenny Ireland, Paul Jesson, Philip L. MacDonald, Sheila Lemon, Suzie Mackenzie, Barbara Mackie, Marina Martin, Richard O'Brien, Stephen Oliver, Gary Olsen, Harold Pinter, Margaret Ramsay, Jane Rayne, Alan Rickman, Dr. P. A. Rixon, A. J. Sayers, Paul Sinclair Brooks, Lindsay Stevens, Richard Stone, Nigel Terry, Mary Trevelyan, Maureen Vincent, Julian Wadham, Julie Walters, Julia M. Walters, Sarah Wheatland.

FOR THE ROYAL COURT

DIRECTION

Artistic Director ..... MAX STAFFORD-CLARK
Deputy Director ..... SIMON CURTIS
Director of the Theatre Upstairs ..... LINDSAY POSNER
Assistant Director ..... PHILIP HOWARD
Casting Director ..... LISA MAKIN
Literary Manager ..... KATE HARWOOD
Senior Script Associate ..... MICHAEL HASTINGS*
Resident Playwright ..... HARWANT S. BAINS*
Artistic Assistant ..... MELANIE KENYON

PRODUCTION

Production Manager ..... BO BARTON
Technical Manager, Theatre Upstairs ..... CHRIS BAGUST
Chief Electrician ..... CHRISTOPHER TOULMIN
Deputy Chief Electrician ..... MARK BRADLEY
Electrician ..... COLIN ROXBOROUGH*
Master Carpenter ..... CHRIS HARDING-ROBERTS
Deputy Carpenter ..... JOHN BURGESS
Costume Supervisor ..... JENNIFER COOK
Wardrobe Assistants ..... IONA KENRICK*, CATHIE SKILBECK

ADMINISTRATION

General Manager ..... GRAHAM COWLEY
Assistant to General Manager ..... LUCY WOOLLATT
Finance Administrator ..... STEPHEN MORRIS
Finance Assistant ..... GILL RUSSELL
Press Manager ..... SALLY LYCETT
Marketing & Publicity Manager ..... GUY CHAPMAN
Development Director ..... TOM PETZAL
Development Assistant ..... JACQUELINE VIEIRA
House Manager ..... GODFREY HAMILTON
Assistant House Manager ..... ALISON SMITH
Bookshop Manager ..... DIANE PETHERICK*
Box Office Manager ..... STEVEN CURRIE
Box Office Assistants ..... GERALD BROOKING, ROSALEEN DEW
Box Office Trainee ..... RITA SHARMA*
Stage Door/Telephonists ..... DIANE PETHERICK*, ANGELA TOULMIN*
Evening Stage Door ..... TYRONE LUCAS*, CERI SHIELDS*
Maintenance ..... JOHN LORRIGIO*
Cleaners ..... EILEEN CHAPMAN*, IVY JONES*, JENNA STORR*
Firemen ..... BEN GOODWIN*, PAUL KLEINMANN*

YOUNG PEOPLE'S THEATRE

Director ..... ELYSE DODGSON
Administrator ..... JANE HELLINGS
Youth Drama Worker ..... SUZY GILMOUR
Schools & Community Liaison Worker ..... MARK HOLNESS
Writer in Residence ..... KARIM ALRAWI*

*Part-time staff

COUNCIL: Chairman: MATTHEW EVANS. CHRIS BAGUST, BO BARTON, STUART BURGE, ANTHONY C. BURTON, CARYL CHURCHILL, BRIAN COX, HARRIET CRUICKSHANK, SIMON CURTIS, ALLAN DAVIS, DAVID LLOYD DAVIS, ROBERT FOX, MRS. HENNY GESTETNER OBE, DEREK GRANGER, DAVID HARE, JOCELYN HERBERT, DAVID KLEEMAN, HANIF KUREISHI, SONIA MELCHETT, JOAN PLOWRIGHT CBE, GREVILLE POKE, JANE RAYNE, JIM TANNER, SIR HUGH WILLATT.

This Theatre is associated with the Thames Television Playwright Scheme, and the Regional Theatre Young Directors Scheme

1707

Ann Pilkington to be privately whipt and imprisoned until she finds out the mother of a bastard child left at Drayton, or gives security for her appearance at next Sessions.

Quarter Sessions Orders, Shropshire.

1755

There were strict laws concerning the 'Poor' at this time, and the case of Jane Morris gives an interesting example of how the law was carried out in the case of an illegitimate child. There is little doubt that her pregnancy came about as a result of the Stretton May Fair jollifications in May 1755. 'Following her Examination and a Complaint by the Churchwardens of Hope Bowdler that her child had been chargeable to the Parish since its birth and would continue to be so, the two Justices of the Peace in the name of His Majesty King George the Second commanded the Petty Constable of Hope Bowdler "to convey ye said Jane Morris from your sd Township of Hope Bowdler to ye House of Correction at Salop and deliver her to the Master thereof and you the sd Master of ye sd House of Correction are hereby required to receive the sd Jane Morris into your sd House and her safely keep to hard labour for one whole year".'

Fordritishope, The Story of a Shropshire Parish.

MELINDA'S NEW HOUSE?

c.1760

'The chastity of women is of all importance, as all property depends on it . . . between a man and his wife, a husband's infidelity is nothing . . . Wise married women don't trouble themselves about infidelity in their husbands . . . The man imposes no bastards upon his wife.'

Dr. Johnson

SHOEMAKERS ROW

1804

At Winchester, two of the party, Andrews and Peters, dressed as countrymen, and, acting as groundbait, went strutting about, playing all manner of pranks. Having attracted some rustics they offered to treat them and retired to a tent where, after a few pots of beer, they declared their intentions of enlisting, Peters spinning out 'a long rigmarole of how his eldest brother, who enlisted that day three years ago, was now a captain in India, as rich as a nabob'. The moment seemed propitious, so one man slipped out for the sergeant, who dropped in as if by accident. Andrews then offered a drink to the sergeant, and shook hands with him, and they all sat down to beer. Andrews formally volunteered to enlist; Peters rose in a jolly, off-hand way and offered to go with him. 'The shilling was put into each of our hands in the king's name and we gave three cheers.' Ten to one but two or three of the company followed suit. If not, the sergeant sat down and pulled out a fistful of money and a couple of watches. Then he presented the watches to the new 'king's men' on behalf of their company, while advancing part of their bounty, adding that there were eight vacancies for sergeants which such smart men could well hope to fill soon. The watches usually had an astonishing effect and secured three or more fish.

Roy Palmer (ed): THE RAMBLING SOLDIER

IN THE LOGGERHEADS INN

1815

'Moreover the weapons they (the officers) and the sergeants carried, swords and halberds, though of little offensive value, were exactly what was needed to keep individual soldiers, or groups of them, from running away. In one of General Lejeune's paintings of a Napoleonic battle in which he fought, he has actually portrayed a French sergeant pushing against the back of one of the French ranks, using his halberd horizontally in both hands to hold the men in place. It is not improbable to think of British sergeants having done the same at Waterloo.'

John Keegan: THE FACE OF BATTLE

PHOTOS OF A TRIP TO SHREWSBURY BY JOHN HAYNES

ON THE TRAIN TO SHREWSBURY

The Royal Court Theatre presents

THE RECRUITING OFFICER

by George Farquhar

MR BALANCE } *Two Justices* ..... MARK LAMBERT
MR SCRUPLE } ..... JUDE AKUWUDIKE
MR WORTHY, *a gentleman of Shropshire* ..... NICK DUNNING
CAPTAIN PLUME, *a recruiting officer* ..... DAVID HAIG
CAPTAIN BRAZEN, *a recruiting officer* ..... RON COOK
KITE, *Sergeant to Plume* ..... JIM BROADBENT
BULLOCK, *a country clown* ..... RON COOK
COSTAR PEARMAIN, *a recruit* ..... JUDE AKUWUDIKE
THOMAS APPLETREE, *a recruit* ..... LINDA BASSETT
PLUCK, *a butcher* ..... MARK LAMBERT
BRIDEWELL, *a constable* ..... NICK DUNNING
SERVANT *to Justice Balance* ..... JUDE AKUWUDIKE

MELINDA, *a lady of fortune* ..... LINDA BASSETT
SILVIA, *daughter to Balance, in love with PLUME* ..... LESLEY SHARP
LUCY, *Melinda's maid* ..... ALPHONSIA EMMANUEL
ROSE, *a country wench* ..... MOSSIE SMITH

ALL OTHER PARTS PLAYED BY MEMBERS OF THE COMPANY

Directed by ..... MAX STAFFORD-CLARK
Designed by ..... PETER HARTWELL
Lighting by ..... ANDY PHILLIPS
Costume Supervisor ..... MARION WEISE
Assistant Director ..... PHILIP HOWARD
Stage Manager ..... NEIL O'MALLEY
Deputy Stage Manager ..... NICOLE GRIFFITHS
Assistant Stage Manager ..... MARK ORMEROD
Poster Design ..... RICHARD WISE
Production Photos ..... JOHN HAYNES

The play takes place in Shrewsbury in the late summer of 1704 following the Battle of Blenheim in August of that year.

There will be one interval of fifteen minutes

Wardrobe care by PERSIL and BIO-TEX. Adhesive by COPYDEX and EVODE LTD. Ioniser for the lighting control room by THE LONDON IONISER CENTRE (836 0211). Cordless drill by MAKITA ELECTRIC (UK) LTD. Watches by THE TIMEX CORPORATION. Batteries by EVER READY, refrigerators by ELECTROLUX and PHILLIPS MAJOR APPLIANCIES LTD. Microwaves by TOSHIBA UK LTD. Kettles for rehearsals by MORPHY RICHARDS. Television for backstage by GRANADA. Video for casting purposes by HITACHI. Sound desk by CADAC. Cold bottled beers at the bar supplied by YOUNG & CO. BREWERY, WANDSWORTH. Coffee machines by CONA.

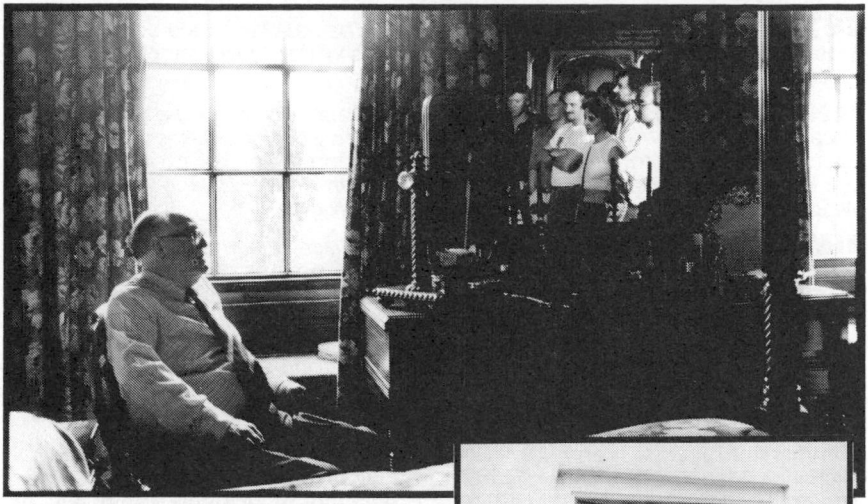

DR DUDLEY IRELAND IN HIS QUEEN ANNE HOUSE (C.1710) OVERLOOKING THE SEVERN

OFF MARKET SQUARE

1706

. . . There was lately published a Comedy call'd 'The Recruiting Officer', to render this employment as odious as possible. Here one 'Captain' is represented as a notorious lyar, another as a Drunkard, one intreagues with Women, another is scandalously guilty of debauching them; and tho' the Serjeant was married to five Women before, yet the Captain persuades him to marry another, as a Cloak for such Roguery, to make up his Five Wives half a Dozen, and to cheat the Queen, by entering a child born on the day before into the Muster-Roll, and after all he stiles these Debaucheries 'an Air of Freedom, which People mistake for Lewdness, as they mistake Formality in others for Religion', and then proceeds in commending his own Practice, and exposing the other. In this Play the Officers are represented as quarrelsome, but Cowards. The Serjeant makes the Mob drunk to list them, gives two of them two Broad Pieces of Gold, for Pictures, and Finding the Money upon them, pretends that they are listed: At another Time he is ready to swear anything for the Good of the Service; and also persuades Men to list in the Disguise of a Conjurer, with most profane Language in Commendation of the Devil; In this Play the Officers confess, that they greatly abuse the new listed Soldiers; Debauching of the Country Wenches is represented as a main Part of the Service; All the Private Centinels are guilty of stealing Horses, Sheep and Fowls, and the Captain desires, that he may have 'but one honest Man in the Company for Novelty's sake'. After this the Justices of the Peace are made the Jest of the Stage, for discharging their duty in listing of soldiers, and the Constable hath a Lash into the Bargain, that no one who serves his Country on this Occasion, may escape the Play-House Censure.

Arthur Bedford: THE EVIL AND DANGER OF STAGE PLAYS

JUDE AKUWUDIKE Recent Theatre: *The Park* (Sheffield Crucible); *Moon on a Rainbow Shawl* (Almeida); Blueprints Writers' Workshop (Soho Poly). Film: *A World Apart.*

LINDA BASSETT Theatre includes: *A Place with the Pigs* (National Theatre); *The Bald Prima Donna, Medea, The Cherry Orchard* (Leicester Haymarket); *Fen* (Joint Stock); Theatre-in-Education (Belgrade, Coventry); for the Royal Court: *Serious Money, Aunt Dan and Lemon.* TV: *Making Waves.* Films: *Waiting for the Moon, Leave to Remain, Paris by Night.*

JIM BROADBENT Theatre includes: *A Place with the Pigs* and *The Government Inspector* (National Theatre); *Ecstasy* (Hampstead); *Goosepimples* (Hampstead/Garrick); *The Messiah, The Complete Guide to Sex, The Greatest Story Ever Told* (National Theatre of Brent); for the Royal Court: *Other Worlds* and *Kafka's Dick.* TV includes: *The Insurance Man, Only Fools and Horses, Birth of a Nation, The Miser.* Films include: *Brazil* and *The Good Father.*

RON COOK Theatre work includes: *Sons of Light, Television Times, The Winter's Tale, The Crucible, The Dillen* (RSC); *She Stoops to Conquer* (Lyric, Hammersmith); *Ecstasy* and *How I Got That Story* (Hampstead); *Cock-Ups* (Royal Exchange, Manchester); *Three Sisters* (Greenwich/Albery); for the Royal Court: *The Arbor, Cloud Nine, The Grass Widow, Greenland.* TV includes: title role in *Richard III, Henry VI* parts 1,2 and 3, *The Merry Wives of Windsor, A Day to Remember, The Singing Detective, The Miser, Bergerac.*

NICK DUNNING Recent Theatre includes: *Richard II, The Wandering Jew, Countrymania* (National Theatre); *The Taming of the Shrew* and *Happy End* (RSC); *A Handful of Dust* and *Marriage* (Shared Experience); for the Royal Court: *Glasshouses.* TV: *The Young Ones, Strangers, Way Upstream, The Firm* (to be shown). Films: *Lamb* and *Remembrance.*

ALPHONSIA EMMANUEL Theatre includes: for the RSC: *The Dillen, Measure for Measure, Camille* (also West End), *Golden Girls, Love's Labour's Lost* and *Goat* (a one-woman show). TV includes: *Give Us a Break* and *Rockcliffe's Babies.* Film: *Sweet Water.*

DAVID HAIG For the Royal Court: 1980 Young Writers' Festival, *The Arbor, Care, Tom and Viv* (London and New York), *Greenland*; for the RSC: *A Midsummer Night's Dream, Volpone, Every Man in His Humour, Worlds Apart, Time of Your Life.* TV includes: *Flame to the Phoenix, Chessgame, Diamonds, Dr. Who, Moonstallion, Blake's Seven.* Films include: *Morons from Outer Space.* Radio includes: *Howard's End, Day Out, Men.*

PETER HARTWELL For the Royal Court: *The Glad Hand, Wheelchair Willie, Not Quite Jerusalem, The Genius, Rat in the Skull, A Colder Climate, The Arbor,* The Edward Bond Season, *Top Girls, Aunt Dan and Lemon, Operation Bad Apple, The Grass Widow, Serious Money.* Theatre Upstairs: *Empty Desk, Marie and Bruce, Seduced.* Joint Stock: *Epsom Downs, Cloud Nine, The Ragged Trousered Philanthropists, Borderline, Crimes of Vautrin.* Lyric, Hammersmith: *She Stoops to Conquer, The Beaux' Stratagem.* NT: *Serjeant Musgrave's Dance.*

MARK LAMBERT Theatre includes: *Red, Black and Ignorant* and *Juno and the Paycock* (RSC); *Observe the Sons of Ulster Marching Towards the Somme* (Abbey Theatre and Hampstead); *Comedians* (Young Vic); *Candy Kisses* (The Bush); for the Royal Court: *Ourselves Alone* and *Built on Sand.* TV includes: *Caught in a Free State, The Young Ones, An Affair in Mind, Time After Time.* Films: *Champions* and *Prayer for the Dying.*

ANDY PHILLIPS Was resident lighting designer at the Royal Court 1965-1972, where he lit over 80 productions; other lighting designs for the Royal Court include: *Women Beware Women, Rat in the Skull,* The Edward Bond Season, *The Last Supper, Greenland.* He designed the lighting for John Dexter's production of *M Butterfly*, currently on Broadway.

LESLEY SHARP Theatre includes: *Macbeth, Maydays, Lear* (RSC); *Six Characters in Search of an Author, Fathers and Sons, Ting Tang Mine, True Dare Kiss, Command or Promise* (National Theatre); *A Family Affair* (Cheek by Jowl); for the Royal Court: *Road, Shirley, Greenland.* TV includes: *Road, Tartuffe, The World of UB40.* Films include: *Rita, Sue and Bob Too* and *The Love Child.*

MOSSIE SMITH Recent theatre includes: *The Crucible* (Young Vic); for the Royal Court: *Shirley* and *Road.* TV includes: *Triangle, Number 10, Reith, Rat in the Skull, Putting on the Ritz, Road* and *A Very Peculiar Practice.*

MAX STAFFORD-CLARK Like George Farquhar, Max Stafford-Clark was educated at Trinity College, Dublin. He has been the Artistic Director of the English Stage Company at the Royal Court since 1980. His contract has recently been renewed for a further period of 3 years.

An Introduction to the Play by Dr. Peter Holland

In 1704 George Farquhar was commissioned as a lieutenant of grenadiers in the infantry regiment which Charles Boyle, fourth Duke of Orrery, had just been empowered to raise for service in Ireland. His decision to enter the army seems to have been primarily economic rather than financial. Though he had had five plays performed in London, only one of them, *The Constant Couple* (first performed in 1699), had been particularly successful. He had married in 1703 and, according to tradition, his wife was not the great heiress she had announced herself to be; whatever the success of the marriage, it did nothing to help Farquhar's finances.

The regiment was formed by a recruitment drive in the summer of 1704, primarily in the West Midlands, with a second bout of recruiting in the following summer (a trip that took Farquhar to Lichfield which was to be the setting for his last play, *The Beaux' Stratagem*). As Orrery himself testified, Farquhar worked extraordinarily hard as a recruiting officer, behaving 'himself with great diligence . . . to the great prejudice of his family'. Since the costs of recruiting were initially paid for out of the recruiting officer's own pocket and since reimbursement of these expenses was always slow in coming, if they were repaid at all, Farquhar's efficiency may have ended up costing him money. When he left the regiment in March 1706 by the usual process of selling his commission, he may have needed the money to pay off the debts of being a good officer. *The Recruiting Officer* was probably written late in 1705; Farquhar showed it to his general, the Duke of Ormonde, Lord Lieutenant of Ireland, and to his colonel, Orrery. Its first performance was at Drury Lane in April 1706.

The formation of regiments like Orrery's was the response to the massive increase in the size of the standing army needed to pursue normal domestic garrison duties and to fight the War of the Spanish Succession, begun in 1702. Maintaining an army at 50,000 was impossible simply by relying on volunteers at a time of comparative economic prosperity. The government took two steps to solve the problem. The Mutiny Act of 1702 allowed convicted criminals to have their prison sentences commuted by being enlisted in the army; the JPs in the play are happy to have a poacher handed over for recruitment. But the expansion of the war into the Spanish Peninsula needed a further measure and the Act for Raising Recruits was passed in 1704. The Act, usually known as the 'Pressing Act', gave wide new powers to all local Justices of the Peace, except those holding military office, to assist recruitment; Farquhar gives Costar Pearmain no higher ambition than to be a Justice of the Peace 'for since this Pressing Act they are greater than any emperor under the sun'.

In particular, JPs were now able to enforce conscription on 'such able-bodied men as have not any lawful calling or employment or visible means for their maintenance and livelihood'. The wording allows Sergeant Kite to argue in the play that a collier should be pressed since he has no '*visible* means of a livelihood'. Local parish constables were to be issued with warrants to collect up any men suspected of being unemployed and bring them before a panel of three JPs who would hand those found guilty of being unemployed over to the army. The payment to all volunteers for the army was two pounds a man — the sum which Plume offers Pearmain and Appletree after Kite has tried to get away with only paying them 'three and twenty shillings and sixpence each'. Pressed recruits received only one pound. More significantly, the parish constable was to be paid 'any sum not exceeding ten shillings' for every man pressed — hence the revelation in the play that the constable let five men go for bribes of 'eleven shillings a man, because he said the Act allows him but ten, so the odd shilling was clear gains'.

Enlistment was accomplished by the payment of money, recording the men's names on the regimental muster roll (the same document on the back of which Kite lists the names of his wives), and the reading of the two crucial sections of the Articles of War which specify the punishments for mutiny and desertion, beginning 'No man shall presume so far as to raise or cause the least mutiny or sedition in the army upon pain of death'.

Landowning gentry, like those in Shrewsbury, had two causes for disliking the war: the recruiting drives played havoc with the availability of farm-workers and the costs of the war were primarily covered by an increase in the land tax to four shillings in the pound. Nonetheless, the huge success of Marlborough's campaigns, with the spectacular victories at Vienna and Blenheim, had induced a state approaching national euphoria in which even the higher war-time rate of taxation was accepted; as Justice Balance comments, 'give us but blood for our money and you shan't want men'. The enthusiasm for British military success was not in any way confined to the gentry, even if the victories did not inspire a rush of volunteers.

It is against this background that Farquhar sets *The Recruiting Officer*. Brecht, in adapting Farquhar's play as *Trumpets and Drums*, set out very deliberately to underline the class basis of war and the horrors of impressment, with its twisting of the law, contrasting England with America — the play's setting is moved to coincide with the American War of Independence. But Farquhar has no such clear-cut intention, even if, from our perspective, the play can be seen as subversively critical of the culture it celebrates. *The Recruiting Officer* is willing to mock the gullibility of the recruits who are, as Farquhar put in his Latin motto on the titlepage of the play's first edition, 'ensnared by wiles and won over by gifts' but the mockery is gentle not contemptuous. The rules of comedy, just as much as the needs of the army, mean that Pearmain and Appletree deserve to be caught. Yet Farquhar finds a real sadness in their refusal to be apart, even while the play is happily relishing the brilliant comic trickery by which Kite and Plume build up their list. While Farquhar may have genuine doubts about the sort of soldiers such methods and the government's legislation were likely to produce (as Plume says, 'let me have one honest man in my company, for the novelty's sake'), the play is in no sense an attack on the war aims for which the abuse-ridden system of recruitment was introduced. Farquhar has no hesitation at all in supporting the war unequivocally. He could rely on the audience's enthusiastic response to Plume's uncomplicated patriotism: 'our general commanded us to beat the French, and we did so; and if he pleases but to say the word, we'll do't again'. *The Recruiting Officer* is scrupulously alert to the tensions created in Shrewsbury by the visits of the recruiting squad. Nonetheless in many ways, not least in the harmony between the army and the gentry, *The Recruiting Officer* envisages an almost utopian image of agreement between provincial society and national policy.

It is precisely in the decision to place *The Recruiting Officer* away from London that Farquhar is at his boldest. Late seventeenth century comedy had rarely been prepared to venture far beyond the fashionable city; as Harriet advises Dorimant in Etherege's *The Man of Mode* (1676), 'I know all beyond High Park's a desert to you'. When plays had moved outside the capital, for example in Thomas Shadwell's *Bury Fair* (1689), the playwrights had used the setting to mock the ridiculous pretensions of provincial society to compete with London, the only true centre of contemporary stylishness. As Millamant says of Sir Wilful Witwoud in Congreve's *The Way of the World* (1700), 'rustic ruder than Gothic' —and Sir Wilful comes from Shrewsbury. When Farquhar has Melinda welcome Silvia to town and complain of the 'smoke, noise, scandal, affectation, and pretension' of Shrewsbury, she speaks as an urban-dweller to whom the fresh air of the Silvia's 'retreat in the country' would in fact be 'intolerable'. Melinda's affectation lies merely in thinking of Shrewsbury as 'town' when the word could only properly mean London. But Farquhar's ridicule of Melinda is vastly outweighed by the play's deep affection for the community of Shrewsbury. Balance's bluff honesty does not ape London styles but it is not in any way ridiculous by comparison. Plume's frequently voiced respect for the country justice is entirely genuine and he uses him as the model for his own future career beyond the end of the play: 'whilst I endeavour by the example of this worthy gentleman to serve my Queen and country at home'.

Plume's willingness to approve such people is of a piece with Farquhar's careful description of him as a man some way away from the conventional model of the Restoration rake. If 'Molly at the castle' was made pregnant by Plume during the last visit of the recruiters to Shrewsbury, Plume does at least provide for his bastard, giving Molly Kite as a husband and using the common contemporary device for increasing a family's income of entering a child on the muster-roll and giving the pay to the mother while the 'soldier' is put on indefinite leave. In terms of Farquhar's own society such actions are the least but also the most that a gentleman might be expected to do to deal with the consequences of an affair with a lower-class woman. While Plume's unconcerned irresponsibility must repel us, the response is not one the play seems to consider. Plume's interest in Rose is purely part of his job: 'kiss the prettiest country wenches, and you are sure of listing the lustiest fellows'. There is no reason to doubt Plume's honesty in his admission to Silvia, disguised as Jack Wilful, that 'I am not that rake the world imagines. I have got an air of freedom, which people mistake for lewdness in me'.

Plume's self-description here is a response to Jack Wilful's surprise at his offer of a share in his bed; it is an offer he makes more than once. It may have been normal for soldiers to sleep two to a bed in barracks but Farquhar is continually fascinated in *The Recruiting Officer* by the nature of male relationships in the army. He does not seek to suggest to any extent that soldiers were actively homosexual (still a capital crime), he is concerned to underline very deliberately the intense physicality of male friendship in the army. Sharing beds and kissing are part of this physical closeness. As Plume and Brazen compete to enlist Jack Wilful, Plume kisses 'him'; Plume and Brazen kiss as they meet; Kite too offers to kiss Wilful:

Silvia. What, men kiss one another!

Kite. We officers do, 'tis our way; we live together like man and wife, always either kissing or fighting.

The replication of civilian heterosexual forms of affection in the all-male analogue world of the army is completely unembarrassed. Farquhar documents and accepts it.

It is a part of his redefinition of the kind of conventional drama from which the main love-plot of the play comes. Melinda may describe Silvia as a 'poor romantic Quixote' and find, at the end of the play, that her 'history is a little romantic' but romantic heroines do not normally find that the country girls like Rose whose virginity they have been protecting are disappointed still to be virgins in the morning.

It is parallelled by the surprising form in which Farquhar explores the relationship of sexual desire between Worthy and Melinda. Worthy's intention to marry Melinda is explicitly a consequence of the economic independence that her inheritance has brought her; since she no longer needs his money his plan of making her his mistress has failed. Marriage is for Worthy a new plan since he cannot seduce Melinda any other way. That Melinda has come dangerously close to becoming his mistress and thereby losing all claims to social respectability in a provincial society like Shrewsbury is something she cannot forget. It is a mark of the sexual double standard that when she reminds Worthy in Act 5 of the means by which 'you would have made me your mistress, that is, your slave' Worthy admits it but can still comment unabashedly in an aside, 'and am sorry I made no better use of 'em'. As Silvia finds when her brother's death leaves her sole heir to her father's fortune of £1,200 a year, a woman's wealth transforms not only her marriage value but also her control over her own desires. Melinda, now rich, can both choose her husband and keep her social position; Silvia, now a wealthy heiress, cannot choose her husband except by strategem and disguise. The device of the woman disguising herself as a man to pursue her lover is found in dozens of Restoration comedies. But while it had previously been the means for the woman to pin down the unfaithful rake, in *The Recruiting Officer* it becomes the means for the woman to outwit her father and society's system of control over a woman as the vehicle for the transmission of inherited wealth.

Throughout the play Farquhar, as one might expect, intertwines the languages of war and of sexual desire. Worthy's attempts on Melinda become a military campaign: ' I did make one general assault, and pushed it with all my forces'. Balance mocks Plume's enquiry about Silvia: ' You're engaged already, wedded to the war; victory is your mistress, and it is below a soldier to think of any other'. In the end the action of the play is resolved when Balance is tricked into consenting to Plume's marrying Silvia by consenting to his enlisting her. The two worlds, the conventional drama of courtship and the new realism of recruiting, profoundly affect each other, far more than the availability of traditionally parallel imagery. Marriage, after all, makes Plume give up his commission.

In his 'Discourse upon Comedy', published in 1702, Farquhar defined comedy as 'a well-framed tale handsomely told, as an agreeable vehicle for counsel or reproof'. *The Recruiting Officer*, in its combination of dramatic energy, provincial realism and cautious questioning of military and sexual *mores*, amply fulfills Farquhar's definition.

Trinity Hall, Cambridge - June 1988

GEORGE FARQUHAR: A BRIEF CHRONOLOGY

1677 Born in Londonderry, son of an impoverished Church of England clergyman.

1689 Presumably still in Londonderry during the Jacobite siege of the city from April to July (and claimed by his mother to have fought in the Battle of the Boyne in 1690).

1694 Entered Trinity College, Dublin, as a 'sizar' — receiving scant board and tuition in return for menial duties.

1696 Left Trinity College without his degree, and acted (indifferently, by all accounts) at the Smock Alley Theatre in Dublin, making his debut as Othello.

1697 Accidentally wounded another actor in a stage duel, and, apparently on the advice of his friend and fellow-actor Robert Wilks, left for London to try his fortune as a playwright.

1698 His first play, the comedy *Love and a Bottle* (published 1699), performed with moderate success at Drury Lane in December, and his anecdotal novella, *Adventures of Covent-Garden*, published anonymously in the same month.

1699 First performance of *The Constant Couple; or, a Trip to the Jubilee* (published 1700) at Drury Lane in November. Credited with the 'discovery' of Anne Oldfield, who created the role of Silvia in *The Recruiting Officer*, in the Mitre tavern.

1700 Contributed to a published collection of *Familiar and Courtly Letters*.

1701 *Sir Harry Wildair*, the unsuccessful sequel to *The Constant Couple*, performed at Drury Lane in April, and published. Contributed to *Letters of Wit, Politicks, and Morality*.

1702 His adaptation of Fletcher's *The Wild Goose Chase* as *The Inconstant* (published 1702) performed at Drury Lane without much success, just before the closing of the theatres for six weeks following the death of William III in March. The satirical comedy *The Twin-Rivals* (published 1703) followed in December, also at Drury Lane, and was an even more pronounced failure. His miscellany of occasional verse and letters, *Love and Business*, published, including the epistolatory *'Discourse upon Comedy'*.

1703 Marriage to Margaret Pemell, a widow with three children, whose poverty apparently surprised him. The short farce *The Stage-Coach* (published 1704), adapted from the French, performed at Lincoln's Inn Fields in December, or January 1704, and became an extremely popular afterpiece.

1704 Commissioned as a Lieutenant of Grenadiers, securing him a small but reliable income of £54 a year. Received almost £100 from a Dublin benefit performance of *The Constant Couple*. Birth of his first daughter, Anne Marguerite.

1705 On recruiting service in Lichfield and Shrewsbury. Birth of his second daughter, Mary.

1706 *The Recruiting Officer* (set in Shrewsbury) performed successfully at Drury Lane in April and published. Well received, but Farquhar was already ill, presumably with tuberculosis, and may have sold his commission to raise money.

1707 *The Beaux' Stratagem* (set in Lichfield) performed at the new theatre in the Haymarket in March, and published. But Farquhar was now gravely ill, and he died in a 'back garret' in St. Martin's Lane in April or May, in his thirtieth year. The funeral was paid for by Wilks, to whom Farquhar entrusted the care of his 'two helpless girls'. Posthumous publication of the unauthorized *Love's Catechism* (largely derived from *The Beaux' Stratagem*) and of the heroic poem *Barcellona*.

CHRONOLOGY COMPILED BY SIMON TRUSSLER

GEORGE FARQUHAR

THE

Recruiting Officer.

A

COMEDY.

As it is Acted at the

THEATRE ROYAL

IN

DRURY-LANE,

By Her MAJESTY's Servants.

Written by Mr. FARQUHAR.

—— *Captique Æolis, doniſque coacti.*
Virg. Lib. II. Æneid.

LONDON:

Printed for BERNARD LINTOTT at the *Croſs Keys* next *Nando's* Coffee-Houſe near *Temple-Bar.*

Price 1*s.* 6*d.*

EPISTLE DEDICATORY

To All Friends Round the Wrekin

My Lords and Gentlemen,

Instead of the mercenary expectations that attend addresses of this nature, I humbly beg, that this may be received as an acknowledgment for the favours you have already conferred. I have transgressed the rules of dedication in offering you anything in that style without first asking your leave; but the entertainment I found in Shropshire commands me to be grateful, and that's all I intend.

'Twas my good fortune to be ordered some time ago into the place which is made the scene of this comedy; I was a perfect stranger to everything in Salop, but its character of loyalty, the number of its inhabitants, the alacrity of the gentlemen in recruiting the army, with their generous and hospitable reception of strangers.

This character I found so amply verified in every particular, that you made recruiting, which is the greatest fatigue upon earth to others, to be the greatest pleasure in the world to me.

The kingdom cannot show better bodies of men, better inclinations for the service, more generosity, more good understanding, nor more politeness, than is to be found at the foot of the Wrekin.

Some little turns of humour that I met with almost within the shade of that famous hill gave the rise to this comedy; and people were apprehensive, that, by the example of some others, I would make the town merry at the expense of the country gentlemen. But they forgot that I was to write a comedy, not a libel; and that whilst I held to nature, no person of any character in your country could suffer by being exposed. I have drawn the justice and the clown in their *puris naturalibus*: the one an apprehensive, sturdy, brave blockhead; and the other a worthy, honest, generous gentleman, hearty in his country's cause, and of as good an understanding as I could give him, which I must confess is far short of his own.

I humbly beg leave to interline a word or two of the adventures of *The Recruiting Officer* upon the stage. Mr Rich, who commands the company for which those recruits were raised, has desired me to acquit him before the world of a charge which he thinks lies heavy upon him for acting this play on Mr Durfey's third night.

Be it known unto all men by these presents, that it was my act and deed, or rather Mr Durfey's; for he *would* play his third night against the first of mine. He brought down a huge flight of frightful birds upon me, when, heaven knows, I had not a feathered fowl in my play except one single Kite; but I presently made Plume a bird, because of his name, and Brazen another, because of the feather in his hat; and with these three I engaged his whole empire, which I think was as great a *wonder* as any *in the sun*.

But to answer his complaints more gravely, the season was far advanced; the officers that made the greatest figures in my play were all commanded to their posts abroad, and waited only for a wind, which might possibly turn in less time than a day; and I know none of Mr Durfey's birds that had posts abroad but his woodcocks, and their season is over; so that he might put off a day with less prejudice than the *Recruiting Officer* could, who has this farther to say for himself, that he was posted before the other spoke, and could not with credit recede from his station.

These and some other rubs this comedy met with before it appeared. But on the other hand, it had powerful helps to set it forward: the Duke of Ormonde encouraged the author, and the Earl of Orrery approved the play. My recruits were reviewed by my general and my colonel, and could not fail to pass muster, and still to add to my success, they were raised among my friends round the Wrekin.

This Health has the advantage over our other celebrated toasts, never to grow worse for the wearing; 'tis a lasting beauty, old without age and common without scandal. That you may live long to set it cheerfully round, and to enjoy the abundant pleasures of your fair and plentiful country, is the hearty wish of,

My Lords and Gentlemen,
Your most obliged,
and most obedient servant,
Geo. Farquhar.

THE PROLOGUE

In ancient times, when Helen's fatal charms
Roused the contending universe to arms,
The Grecian council happily deputes
The sly Ulysses forth – to raise recruits.
The artful captain found, without delay, 5
Where great Achilles, a deserter, lay.
Him Fate had warned to shun the Trojan blows;
Him Greece required – against their Trojan foes.
All the recruiting arts were needful here
To raise this great, this tim'rous volunteer. 10
Ulysses well could talk – he stirs, he warms
The warlike youth. He listens to the charms
Of plunder, fine laced coats, and glitt'ring arms.
Ulysses caught the young aspiring boy,
And listed him who wrought the fate of Troy. 15
Thus by recruiting was bold Hector slain;
Recruiting thus fair Helen did regain.
If for one Helen such prodigious things
Were acted, that they even listed kings;
If for one Helen's artful, vicious charms, 20
Half the transported world was found in arms;
What for so many Helens may we dare,
Whose minds, as well as faces, are so fair?
If, by one Helen's eyes, old Greece could find
Its Homer fired to write – even Homer blind, 25
The Britons sure beyond compare may write,
That view so many Helens every night.

THE RECRUITING OFFICER

Act I, Scene i

The Market-place
DRUMMER *beats the 'Grenadier March'*
Enter SERGEANT KITE, *followed by the* MOB

KITE (*Making a speech*)
If any gentlemen soldiers, or others, have a mind to serve Her Majesty, and pull down the French king; if any prentices have severe masters, any children have undutiful parents; if any servants have too little wages, or any husband too much wife; let them repair to the noble Sergeant Kite, at the Sign of the Raven, in this good town of Shrewsbury, and they shall receive present relief and entertainment. – Gentlemen, I don't beat my drums here to ensnare or inveigle any man; for you must know, gentlemen, that I am a man of honour. Besides, I don't beat up for common soldiers; no, I list only grenadiers, grenadiers, gentlemen – pray, gentlemen, observe this cap – this is the cap of honour, it dubs a man a gentleman in the drawing of a tricker; and he that has the good fortune to be born six foot high was born to be a great man. (*To one of the Mob*) Sir, will you give me leave to try this cap upon your head?

MOB
Is there no harm in't? Won't the cap list me?

KITE
No, no, no more than I can, – come, let me see how it becomes you.

MOB
Are you sure there be no conjuration in it, no gunpowder plot upon me?

KITE
No, no, friend; don't fear, man.

MOB
My mind misgives me plaguily – let me see it. (*Going to put it on*) It smells woundily of sweat and brimstone; pray, Sergeant, what writing is this upon the face of it?

KITE
'The Crown, or the Bed of Honour'.

MOB

Pray now, what may be that same bed of honour?

KITE

Oh, a mighty large bed, bigger by half than the great bed of Ware, ten thousand people may lie in't together and never feel one another.

MOB

My wife and I would do well to lie in't, for we don't care for feeling one another – but do folk sleep sound in this same bed of honour?

KITE

Sound! Aye, so sound that they never wake.

MOB

Wauns! I wish again that my wife lay there.

KITE

Say you so? Then I find, brother –

MOB

Brother! Hold there, friend, I'm no kindred to you that I know of, as yet – look'ee, Sergeant, no coaxing, no wheedling, d'ye see; if I have a mind to list, why so – if not, why 'tis not so – therefore take your cap and your brothership back again, for I an't disposed at this present writing – no coaxing, no brothering me, faith.

KITE

I coax! I wheedle! I'm above it. Sir, I have served twenty campaigns. But sir, you talk well, and I must own that you are a man every inch of you, a pretty, young, sprightly fellow – I love a fellow with a spirit, but I scorn to coax, 'tis base; though I must say that never in my life have I seen a man better built; how firm and strong he treads, he steps like a castle! But I scorn to wheedle any man – come, honest lad, will you take share of a pot?

MOB

Nay, for that matter, I'll spend my penny with the best he that wears a head, that is, begging your pardon, sir, and in a fair way.

KITE

Give me your hand then; and now, gentlemen, I have no more to say but this – here's a purse of gold, and there is a tub of humming ale at my quarters; 'tis the Queen's money and the Queen's drink. She's a generous queen and loves her subjects – I hope, gentlemen, you won't refuse the Queen's health?

ALL MOB
No, no, no.

KITE
Huzza then! Huzza for the Queen, and the honour of Shropshire!

ALL MOB
Huzza!

KITE
Beat drum.

Exeunt, drummer beating the 'Grenadier March'

Enter PLUME *in a riding habit*

PLUME
By the Grenadier March that should be my drum, and by that shout it should beat with success – let me see – (*looks on his watch*) – four o'clock – at ten yesterday morning I left London – a hundred and twenty miles in thirty hours is pretty smart riding, but nothing to the fatigue of recruiting.

Enter KITE

KITE
Welcome to Shrewsbury, noble Captain: from the banks of the Danube to the Severn side, noble Captain, you're welcome.

PLUME
A very elegant reception indeed, Mr Kite, I find you are fairly entered into your recruiting strain – pray, what success?

KITE
I have been here but a week and I have recruited five.

PLUME
Five! Pray, what are they?

KITE
I have listed the strong man of Kent, the king of the gypsies, a Scotch pedlar, a scoundrel attorney, and a Welsh parson.

PLUME
An attorney! Wert thou mad? List a lawyer! Discharge him, discharge him this minute.

KITE
Why, sir?

PLUME
Because I will have nobody in my company that can write; a fellow that can write, can draw petitions – I say, this minute discharge him.

KITE

And what shall I do with the parson?

PLUME

Can he write?

KITE

Umh – he plays rarely upon the fiddle.

PLUME

Keep him by all means. But how stands the country affected? Were the people pleased with the news of my coming to town?

KITE

Sir, the mob are so pleased with your honour, and the justices and better sort of people are so delighted with me, that we shall soon do our business. But, sir, you have got a recruit here that you little think of.

PLUME

Who?

KITE

One that you beat up for last time you were in the country: You remember your old friend Molly at the Castle?

PLUME

She's not with child, I hope.

KITE

No, no, sir; she was brought to bed yesterday.

PLUME

Kite, you must father the child.

KITE

Humph – and so her friends will oblige me to marry the mother.

PLUME

If they should, we'll take her with us, she can wash, you know, and make a bed upon occasion.

KITE

Aye, or unmake it upon occasion. But your honour knows that I'm married already.

PLUME

To how many?

KITE

I can't tell readily – I have set them down here upon the back of the muster-roll. (*Draws it out*) Let me see – *Imprimis*, Mrs Sheely Snickereyes, she sells potatoes upon Ormonde Quay in Dublin – Peggy Guzzle, the brandy-woman at the Horse-guard at Whitehall – Dolly Waggon, the carrier's daughter in Hull – Mademoiselle Van-bottom-flat at the

Buss – then Jenny Oakum, the ship-carpenter's widow at Portsmouth; but I don't reckon upon her, for she was married at the same time to two lieutenants of marines, and a man of war's boatswain. 115

PLUME

A full company – you have named five – come, make 'em half a dozen, Kite. Is the child a boy or a girl? 120

KITE

A chopping boy.

PLUME

Then set the mother down in your list, and the boy in mine; enter him a grenadier by the name of Francis Kite, absent upon furlough – I'll allow you a man's pay for his subsistence; and now go comfort the wench in the straw. 125

KITE

I shall, sir.

PLUME

But hold, have you made any use of your German doctor's habit since you arrived?

KITE

Yes, yes, sir; and my fame's all about the country for the most faithful fortune-teller that ever told a lie; I was obliged to let my landlord into the secret for the convenience of keeping it so, but he's an honest fellow and will be trusty to any roguery that is confided to him. This device, sir, will get you men, and me money, which I think is all we want at present – but yonder comes your friend Mr Worthy – has your honour any farther commands? 130 135

PLUME

None at present. *Exit* KITE

'Tis indeed the picture of Worthy, but the life's departed.

Enter WORTHY

PLUME

What, arms a-cross, Worthy! Methinks you should hold 'em open when a friend's so near. The man has got the vapours in his ears, I believe; I must expel this melancholy spirit. 140

Spleen, thou worst of fiends below,
Fly, I conjure thee by this magic blow.

Slaps WORTHY *on the shoulder*

WORTHY

Plume! My dear Captain, welcome. Safe and sound returned!

PLUME

I 'scaped safe from Germany, and sound, I hope, from 145

London: you see I have lost neither leg, arm nor nose; then for my inside, 'tis neither troubled with sympathies nor antipathies, and I have an excellent stomach for roast beef.

WORTHY

Thou art a happy fellow; once I was so.

PLUME

What ails thee, man? No inundations nor earthquakes in Wales, I hope? Has your father rose from the dead, and reassumed his estate?

WORTHY

No.

PLUME

Then you are married, surely.

WORTHY

No.

PLUME

Then you are mad, or turning Quaker.

WORTHY

Come, I must out with it – your once gay, roving friend is dwindled into an obsequious, thoughtful, romantic, constant coxcomb.

PLUME

And pray, what is all this for?

WORTHY

For a woman.

PLUME

Shake hands, brother, if you go to that – behold me as obsequious, as thoughtful, and as constant a coxcomb as your worship.

WORTHY

For whom?

PLUME

For a regiment. – But for a woman! 'Sdeath! I have been constant to fifteen at a time, but never melancholy for one; and can the love of one bring you into this pickle? Pray, who is this miraculous Helen?

WORTHY

A Helen indeed, not to be won under a ten years' siege; as great a beauty, and as great a jilt.

PLUME

A jilt! Pho! Is she as great a whore?

WORTHY

No, no.

PLUME
'Tis ten thousand pities; but who is she? Do I know her?
WORTHY
Very well. 175
PLUME
Impossible! – I know no woman that will hold out a ten years' siege.
WORTHY
What think you of Melinda?
PLUME
Melinda! Why, she began to capitulate this time twelve-month, and offered to surrender upon honourable terms; 180 and I advised you to propose a settlement of five hundred pound a year to her, before I went last abroad.
WORTHY
I did, and she hearkened to't, desiring only one week to consider; when beyond her hopes the town was relieved, and I forced to turn my siege into a blockade. 185
PLUME
Explain, explain.
WORTHY
My Lady Richly, her aunt in Flintshire, dies, and leaves her at this critical time twenty thousand pound.
PLUME
Oh, the devil! What a delicate woman was there spoiled! But by the rules of war now, Worthy, blockade was foolish – 190 after such a convoy of provisions was entered the place, you could have no thought of reducing it by famine – you should have redoubled your attacks, taken the town by storm, or have died upon the breach.
WORTHY
I did make one general assault, and pushed it with all my 195 forces; but I was so vigorously repulsed, that despairing of ever gaining her for a mistress, I have altered my conduct, given my addresses the obsequious and distant turn, and court her now for a wife.
PLUME
So, as you grew obsequious, she grew haughty, and because 200 you approached her as a goddess, she used you like a dog.
WORTHY
Exactly.
PLUME
'Tis the way of 'em all. Come, Worthy, your obsequious and distant airs will never bring you together; you must not think

to surmount her pride by your humility. Would you bring her to better thoughts of you, she must be reduced to a meaner opinion of herself – let me see – the very first thing that I would do, should be to lie with her chambermaid, and hire three or four wenches in the neighbourhood to report that I had got them with child. Suppose we lampooned all the pretty women in town, and left her out? Or what if we made a ball, and forgot to invite her, with one or two of the ugliest?

WORTHY

These would be mortifications, I must confess; but we live in such a precise, dull place that we can have no balls, no lampoons, no –

PLUME

What! No bastards! And so many recruiting officers in town; I thought 'twas a maxim among them to leave as many recruits in the country as they carried out.

WORTHY

Nobody doubts your goodwill, noble Captain, in serving your country with your best blood: witness our friend Molly at the Castle, – there have been tears in town about that business, Captain.

PLUME

I hope Silvia has not heard of't.

WORTHY

Oh sir, have you thought of her? I began to fancy you had forgot poor Silvia.

PLUME

Your affairs had put mine quite out of my head. 'Tis true, Silvia and I had once agreed to go to bed together, could we have adjusted preliminaries; but she would have the wedding before consummation, and I was for consummation before the wedding – we could not agree. She was a pert obstinate fool, and would lose her maidenhead her own way, so she may keep it for Plume.

WORTHY

But do you intend to marry upon no other conditions?

PLUME

Your pardon, sir, I'll marry upon no condition at all, – if I should, I'm resolved never to bind myself to a woman for my whole life, till I know whether I shall like her company for half an hour. Suppose I married a woman that wanted a leg? Such a thing might be, unless I examined the goods beforehand. If people would but try one another's constitutions before they engaged, it would prevent all these elopements, divorces, and the devil knows what.

WORTHY

Nay, for that matter, the town did not stick to say, that –

PLUME

I hate country towns for that reason – if your town has a dishonourable thought of Silvia, it deserves to be burnt to the ground. – I love Silvia, I admire her frank, generous disposition; there's something in that girl more than woman, her sex is but a foil to her – the ingratitude, dissimulation, envy, pride, avarice, and vanity of her sister females, do but set off their contraries in her – in short, were I once a general, I would marry her.

WORTHY

Faith, you have reason; for were you but a corporal, she would marry you. But my Melinda coquettes it with every fellow she sees – I lay fifty pound she makes love to you.

PLUME

I'll lay fifty pound that I return it if she does – look'ee, Worthy, I'll win her and give her to you afterwards.

WORTHY

If you win her you shall wear her, faith; I would not give a fig for the conquest without the credit of the victory.

Enter KITE

KITE

Captain, Captain, a word in your ear.

PLUME

You may speak out, here are none but friends.

KITE

You know, sir, that you sent me to comfort the good woman in the straw, Mrs Molly – my wife, Mr Worthy.

WORTHY

Oho! Very well – I wish you joy, Mr Kite.

KITE

Your worship very well may – for I have got both a wife and a child in half an hour – but as I was a-saying, you sent me to comfort Mrs Molly – my wife, I mean – but what d'ye think, sir? She was better comforted before I came.

PLUME

As how?

KITE

Why, sir, a footman in a blue livery had brought her ten guineas to buy her baby clothes.

PLUME

Who in the name of wonder could send them?

KITE

Nay, sir, I must whisper that – (*Whispers*) Mrs Silvia.

PLUME

Silvia! Generous creature.

WORTHY

Silvia! Impossible.

KITE

Here be the guineas, sir; I took the gold as part of my wife's portion. Nay, farther, sir, she sent word the child should be taken all imaginable care of, and that she intended to stand godmother. The same footman, as I was coming to you with this news, called after me, and told me that his lady would speak with me – I went, and upon hearing that you were come to town, she gave me half a guinea for the news, and ordered me to tell you, that Justice Balance, her father, who is just come out of the country, would be glad to see you.

PLUME

There's a girl for you, Worthy – is there anything of woman in this? No, 'tis noble and generous, manly friendship; show me another woman that would lose an inch of her prerogative that way, without tears, fits, and reproaches. The common jealousy of her sex, which is nothing but their avarice of pleasure, she despises; and can part with the lover, though she dies for the man. – Come, Worthy, where's the best wine? For there I'll quarter.

WORTHY

Horton has a fresh pipe of choice Barcelona, which I would not let him pierce before, because I reserved the maidenhead of it for your welcome to town.

PLUME

Let's away then – Mr Kite, wait on the lady with my humble service, and tell her I shall only refresh a little, and wait upon her.

WORTHY

Hold, Kite – have you seen the other recruiting captain?

KITE

No, sir.

PLUME

Another? Who is he?

WORTHY

My rival in the first place, and the most unaccountable fellow; but I'll tell you more as we go. *Exeunt*

[Act I], Scene ii

MELINDA's *Apartment*
MELINDA *and* SILVIA *meeting*

MELINDA

Welcome to town, cousin Silvia. (*Salute*) I envied you your retreat in the country; for Shrewsbury, methinks, and all your heads of shires, are the most irregular places for living; here we have smoke, noise, scandal, affectation, and pretension; in short, everything to give the spleen, and nothing to divert it – then the air is intolerable.

SILVIA

Oh, madam, I have heard the town commended for its air.

MELINDA

But you don't consider, Silvia, how long I have lived in't! For I can assure you, that to a lady the least nice in her constitution, no air can be good above half a year; change of air I take to be the most agreeable of any variety in life.

SILVIA

As you say, cousin Melinda, there are several sorts of airs: airs in conversation, airs in behaviour, airs in dress; then we have our quality airs, our sickly airs, our reserved airs, and sometimes our impudent airs.

MELINDA

Psha! I talk only of the air we breathe or more properly of that we taste – have not you, Silvia, found a vast difference in the taste of airs?

SILVIA

Pray, cousin, are not vapours a sort of air? Taste air! You might as well tell me I may feed on air. But prithee, my dear Melinda, don't put on such an air to me; your education and mine were just the same, and I remember the time when we never troubled our heads about air, but when the sharp air from the Welsh mountains made our noses drop in a cold morning at the boarding-school.

MELINDA

Our education, cousin, was the same, but our temperaments had nothing alike; you have the constitution of a horse –

SILVIA

So far as to be troubled with neither spleen, colic, nor vapours; I need no salt for my stomach, no hartshorn for my head, nor wash for my complexion; I can gallop all the morning after the hunting-horn, and all the evening after a fiddle. In short, I can do everything with my father but drink and shoot flying; and I'm sure I can do everything my mother could, were I put to the trial.

MELINDA

You're in a fair way of being put to't; for I'm told your captain is come to town.

SILVIA

Aye, Melinda, he is come, and I'll take care he shan't go without a companion.

MELINDA

You're certainly mad, cousin.

SILVIA

And there's a pleasure, sure, in being mad,
Which none but madmen know.

MELINDA

Thou poor, romantic Quixote, hast thou the vanity to imagine that a young, sprightly officer that rambles o'er half the globe in half a year, can confine his thoughts to the little daughter of a country justice in an obscure corner of the world?

SILVIA

Pshaw! What care I for his thoughts? I should not like a man with confined thoughts, it shows a narrowness of soul. Constancy is but a dull, sleepy quality at best, they will hardly admit it among the manly virtues; nor do I think it deserves a place with bravery, knowledge, policy, justice, and some other qualities that are proper to that noble sex. In short, Melinda, I think a petticoat a mighty simple thing, and I'm heartily tired of my sex.

MELINDA

That is, you are tired of an appendix to our sex, that you can't so handsomely get rid of in petticoats as if you were in breeches. O'my conscience, Silvia, hadst thou been a man, thou hadst been the greatest rake in Christendom.

SILVIA

I should endeavour to know the world, which a man can never do thoroughly without half a hundred friendships, and as many amours. But now I think on't, how stands your affair with Mr Worthy?

MELINDA

He's my aversion.

SILVIA

Vapours!

MELINDA
What do you say, madam?

SILVIA
I say that you should not use that honest fellow so inhumanely. He's a gentleman of parts and fortune, and beside that he's my Plume's friend, and by all that's sacred, if you don't use him better, I shall expect satisfaction.

MELINDA
Satisfaction! You begin to fancy yourself in breeches in good earnest. But to be plain with you, I like Worthy the worse for being so intimate with your captain, for I take him to be a loose, idle, unmannerly coxcomb.

SILVIA
Oh, madam! You never saw him, perhaps, since you were mistress of twenty thousand pound; you only knew him when you were capitulating with Worthy for a settlement, which perhaps might encourage him to be a little loose and unmannerly with you.

MELINDA
What do you mean, madam?

SILVIA
My meaning needs no interpretation, madam.

MELINDA
Better it had, madam, for methinks you're too plain.

SILVIA
If you mean the plainness of my person, I think your ladyship as plain as me to the full.

MELINDA
Were I assured of that, I should be glad to take up with a rakehelly officer as you do.

SILVIA
Again! Look'ee, madam – you're in your own house.

MELINDA
And if you had kept in yours, I should have excused you.

SILVIA
Don't be troubled, madam, I shan't desire to have my visit returned.

MELINDA
The sooner therefore you make an end of this the better.

SILVIA
I'm easily advised to follow my inclinations – so, madam – your humble servant. *Exit*

MELINDA
Saucy thing!

Enter LUCY

LUCY
What's the matter, madam?

MELINDA
Did you not see the proud nothing, how she swells upon the arrival of her fellow? 95

LUCY
Her fellow has not been long enough arrived to occasion any great swelling, madam; I don't believe she has seen him yet.

MELINDA
Nor shan't if I can help it; let me see – I have it – bring me pen and ink – hold, I'll go write in my closet. 100

LUCY
An answer to this letter, I hope, madam. (*Presents a letter*)

MELINDA
Who sent it?

LUCY
Your captain, madam.

MELINDA
He's a fool, and I'm tired of him, send it back unopened.

LUCY
The messenger's gone, madam. 105

MELINDA
Then how shall I send an answer? Call him back immediately, while I go write. *Exeunt*

Act II, Scene i

An Apartment [*in* JUSTICE BALANCE'*s House*]
Enter JUSTICE BALANCE *and* PLUME

BALANCE
Look'ee, Captain, give us but blood for our money, and you shan't want men. I remember that for some years of the last war we had no blood nor wounds but in the officers' mouths, nothing for our millions but newspapers not worth a reading – our armies did nothing but play at prison bars and hide-and-seek with the enemy; but now ye have brought us colours and standards and prisoners; odsmylife, Captain, get us but another Marshal of France, and I'll go myself for a soldier. 5

PLUME
Pray, Mr Balance, how does your fair daughter? 10

BALANCE

Ah, Captain, what is my daughter to a Marshal of France? We're upon a nobler subject. I want to have a particular description of the Battle of Höchstädt.

PLUME

The battle, sir, was a very pretty battle as one should desire to see, but we were all so intent upon victory that we never minded the battle; all that I know of the matter is, our general commanded us to beat the French, and we did so, and if he pleases to say the word, we'll do't again. – But pray, sir, how does Mrs Silvia?

BALANCE

Still upon Silvia! For shame, Captain – you're engaged already, wedded to the war; victory is your mistress, and it is below a soldier to think of any other.

PLUME

As a mistress, I confess, but as a friend, Mr Balance.

BALANCE

Come, come, Captain, never mince the matter, would not you debauch my daughter if you could?

PLUME

How, sir! I hope she's not to be debauched.

BALANCE

Faith, but she is, sir, and any woman in England of her age and complexion, by a man of your youth and vigour. Look'ee, Captain, once I was young and once an officer as you are, and I can guess at your thoughts now by what mine were then, and I remember very well, that I would have given one of my legs to have deluded the daughter of an old, plain country gentleman, as like me as I was then like you.

PLUME

But, sir, was that country gentleman your friend and benefactor?

BALANCE

Not much of that.

PLUME

There the comparison breaks; the favours, sir, that –

BALANCE

Pho, I hate speeches. If I have done you any service, Captain, 'twas to please myself, for I love thee; and if I could part with my girl, you should have her as soon as any young fellow I know; I hope you have more honour than to quit the service, and she more prudence than to follow the camp. But she's at her own disposal, she has fifteen hundred pound in her pocket, and so – Silvia, Silvia! *Calls*

Enter SILVIA

SILVIA

There are some letters, sir, come by the post from London; I left them upon the table in your closet.

BALANCE

And here is a gentleman from Germany. (*Presents* PLUME *to her*) Captain, you'll excuse me, I'll go read my letters, and wait on you. *Exit*

SILVIA

Sir, you're welcome to England.

PLUME

You are indebted to me a welcome, madam, since the hopes of receiving it from this fair hand was the principal cause of my seeing England.

SILVIA

I have often heard that soldiers were sincere, shall I venture to believe public report?

PLUME

You may, when 'tis backed by private insurance; for I swear, madam, by the honour of my profession, that whatever dangers I went upon, it was with the hope of making myself more worthy of your esteem, and if I ever had thoughts of preserving my life, 'twas for the pleasure of dying at your feet.

SILVIA

Well, well, you shall die at my feet, or where you will; but you know, sir, there is a certain will and testament to be made beforehand.

PLUME

My will, madam, is made already, and there it is. (*Gives her a parchment*) And if you please to open that parchment, which was drawn the evening before the Battle of Blenheim, you will find whom I left my heir.

SILVIA *opens the will and reads*

SILVIA

'Mrs Silvia Balance'. – Well, Captain, this is a handsome and a substantial compliment; but I can assure you I am much better pleased with the bare knowledge of your intention than I should have been in the possession of your legacy; but methinks, sir, you should have left something to your little boy at the Castle.

PLUME

(*Aside*) That's home. – My little boy! Lack-a-day, madam, that alone may convince you 'twas none of mine; why the girl, madam, is my sergeant's wife, and so the poor creature gave out that I was father in hopes that my friends might support her in case of necessity; that was all, madam. – My boy! No, no, no.

Enter SERVANT

SERVANT

Madam, my master has received some ill news from London and desires to speak with you immediately, and he begs the captain's pardon that he can't wait on him as he promised.

PLUME

Ill news! Heavens avert it; nothing could touch me nearer than to see that generous, worthy gentleman afflicted; I'll leave you to comfort him, and be assured that if my life and fortune can be any way serviceable to the father of my Silvia, he shall freely command both.

SILVIA

The necessity must be very pressing that would engage me to endanger either. *Exeunt severally*

[Act II], Scene ii

Another Apartment

Enter BALANCE *and* SILVIA

SILVIA

Whilst there is life there is hope, sir; perhaps my brother may recover.

BALANCE

We have but little reason to expect it. Dr Kilman acquaints me here, that before this comes to my hands he fears I shall have no son. – Poor Owen! But the decree is just; I was pleased with the death of my father, because he left me an estate, and now I'm punished with the loss of an heir to inherit mine. I must now look upon you as the only hopes of my family, and I expect that the augmentation of your fortune will give you fresh thoughts and new prospects.

SILVIA

My desire of being punctual in my obedience requires that you would be plain in your commands, sir.

BALANCE

The death of your brother makes you sole heiress to my estate, which you know is about twelve hundred pounds a year; this fortune gives you a fair claim to quality and a title; you must set a just value upon yourself, and in plain terms think no more of Captain Plume.

SILVIA

You have often commended the gentleman, sir.

BALANCE

And I do so still; he's a very pretty fellow; but though I liked him well enough for a bare son-in-law, I don't approve of him for an heir to my estate and family; fifteen hundred pound, indeed, I might trust in his hands, and it might do the young fellow a kindness, but odsmylife, twelve hundred pound a year would ruin him, quite turn his brain. A captain of foot worth twelve hundred pound a year! 'Tis a prodigy in nature. Besides this, I have five or six thousand pounds in woods upon my estate; oh, that would make him stark mad! For you must know that all captains have a mighty aversion to timber, they can't endure to see trees standing. Then I should have some rogue of a builder by the help of his damned magic art transform my noble oaks and elms into cornishes, portals, sashes, birds, beasts, gods, and devils, to adorn some maggoty, new-fashioned bauble upon the Thames; and then you should have a dog of a gardener bring a *habeas corpus* for my *terra firma*, remove it to Chelsea or Twit'nam, and clap it into grass-plats and gravel walks.

Enter a SERVANT

SERVANT

Sir, here's one below with a letter for your worship, but he will deliver it into no hands but your own.

BALANCE

Come, show me the messenger. *Exit with* SERVANT

SILVIA

Make the dispute between love and duty, and I am Prince Prettyman exactly. – If my brother dies, ah, poor brother! If he lives, ah, poor sister! – 'Tis bad both ways; I'll try it again, – follow my own inclinations and break my father's heart, or obey his commands and break my own; worse and worse. Suppose I take it thus – a moderate fortune, a pretty fellow, and a pad; or a fine estate, a coach-and-six, and an ass – that will never do neither.

Enter BALANCE *and* SERVANT

BALANCE
Put four horses into the coach.
To the SERVANT, *who goes out*
Ho, Silvia –

SILVIA
Sir.

BALANCE
How old were you when your mother died?

SILVIA
So young that I don't remember I ever had one; and you have been so careful, so indulgent to me since, that indeed I never wanted one.

BALANCE
Have I ever denied you anything you asked of me?

SILVIA
Never, that I remember.

BALANCE
Then, Silvia, I must beg that once in your life you would grant me a favour.

SILVIA
Why should you question it, sir?

BALANCE
I don't, but I would rather counsel than command; I don't propose this with the authority of a parent, but as the advice of your friend, that you would take the coach this moment and go into the country.

SILVIA
Does this advice, sir, proceed from the contents of the letter you received just now?

BALANCE
No matter; I will be with you in three or four days and then give you my reasons. But before you go, I expect you will make me one solemn promise.

SILVIA
Propose the thing, sir.

BALANCE
That you will never dispose of yourself to any man without my consent.

SILVIA
I promise.

BALANCE
Very well, and to be even with you, I promise I will never

dispose of you without your own consent; and so, Silvia, the coach is ready; farewell. (*Leads her to the door and returns*) Now she's gone, I'll examine the contents of this letter a little nearer. (*Reads*)

Sir,

My intimacy with Mr Worthy has drawn a secret from him that he had from his friend Captain Plume, and my friendship and relation to your family oblige me to give you timely notice of it: the captain has dishonourable designs upon my cousin Silvia. Evils of this nature are more easily prevented than amended, and that you would immediately send my cousin into the country is the advice of,

Sir, your humble servant,

MELINDA.

Why, the devil's in the young fellows of this age; they're ten times worse than they were in my time! Had he made my daughter a whore and forswore it like a gentleman, I could have almost pardoned it; but to tell tales beforehand is monstrous! Hang it, I can fetch down a woodcock or snipe, and why not a hat and feather? I have a case of good pistols, and have a good mind to try.

Enter WORTHY

BALANCE

Worthy, your servant.

WORTHY

I'm sorry, sir, to be the messenger of ill news.

BALANCE

I apprehend it, sir; you have heard that my son Owen is past recovery.

WORTHY

My advices say he's dead, sir.

BALANCE

He's happy, and I am satisfied; the strokes of heaven I can bear; but injuries from men, Mr Worthy, are not so easily supported.

WORTHY

I hope, sir, you're under no apprehension of wrong from anybody?

BALANCE

You know I ought to be.

WORTHY

You wrong my honour, sir, in believing I could know anything to your prejudice without resenting it as much as you should.

BALANCE

This letter, sir, which I tear in pieces to conceal the person that sent it, informs me that Plume has a design upon Silvia, and that you are privy to't.

WORTHY

Nay then, sir, I must do myself justice and endeavour to find out the author. (*Takes up a bit*) Sir, I know the hand, and if you refuse to discover the contents, Melinda shall tell me. *Going*

BALANCE

Hold, sir, the contents I have told you already, only with this circumstance, that her intimacy with Mr Worthy had drawn the secret from him.

WORTHY

Her intimacy with me! – Dear sir, let me pick up the pieces of this letter; 'twill give me such a hank upon her pride, to have her own an intimacy under her hand; 'twas the luckiest accident. (*Gathering up the letter*) The aspersion, sir, was nothing but malice, the effect of a little quarrel between her and Mrs Silvia.

BALANCE

Are you sure of that, sir?

WORTHY

Her maid gave me the history of part of the battle just now, as she overheard it.

BALANCE

'Tis probable, I am satisfied.

WORTHY

But I hope, sir, your daughter has suffered nothing upon the account?

BALANCE

No, no – poor girl, she's so afflicted with the news of her brother's death that to avoid company she begged leave to be gone into the country.

WORTHY

And is she gone?

BALANCE

I could not refuse her, she was so pressing; the coach went from the door the minute before you came.

WORTHY

So pressing to be gone, sir! – I find her fortune will give her the same airs with Melinda, and then Plume and I may laugh at one another.

BALANCE

Like enough; women are as subject to pride as we are, and why mayn't great women as well as great men forget their old acquaintance? But come, where's this young fellow? I love him so well it would break the heart of me to think him a rascal. – (*Aside*) I'm glad my daughter's gone fairly off though. – Where does the captain quarter?

WORTHY

At Horton's; I'm to meet him there two hours hence, and we should be glad of your company.

BALANCE

Your pardon, dear Worthy, I must allow a day or two to the death of my son; the decorum of mourning is what we owe the world because they pay it to us. Afterwards, I'm yours over a bottle, or how you will.

WORTHY

Sir, I'm your humble servant. *Exeunt severally*

[Act II], Scene iii

The Street

Enter KITE, [*leading* COSTAR PEARMAIN *in one hand, and* THOMAS APPLETREE *in the other, both drunk*]

KITE (*Sings*)

Our prentice Tom may now refuse
To wipe his scoundrel master's shoes,
For now he's free to sing and play,
Over the hills and far away.
Over, &c.

[APPLETREE *and* PEARMAIN *join in the chorus*]

We all shall lead more happy lives,
By getting rid of brats and wives,
That scold and brawl both night and day,
Over the hills and far away.
Over, &c.

Hey, boys! Thus we soldiers live; drink, sing, dance, play; we live, as one should say – we live – 'tis impossible to tell how we live. We're all princes – why – why, you're a king – you're an emperor, and I'm a prince – now – an't we? –

APPLETREE

No, Sergeant – I'll be no emperor.

KITE
No?
APPLETREE
No, I'll be a justice of peace.
KITE
A justice of peace, man!
APPLETREE
Aye, wauns will I, for since this Pressing Act they are greater than any emperor under the sun.
KITE
Done; you're a justice of peace, and you're a king, and I'm a duke, and a rum duke, an't I?
PEARMAIN
No, but I'll be no king.
KITE
What then?
PEARMAIN
I'll be a queen.
KITE
A queen!
PEARMAIN
Aye, Queen of England, that's greater than any king of 'em all.
KITE
Bravely said, faith! Huzza for the Queen! *All huzza*
But hark'ee you Mr Justice and you Mr Queen, did you ever see the Queen's picture?
BOTH
No, no, no.
KITE
I wonder at that; I have two of 'em set in gold, and as like Her Majesty, God bless the mark. (*He takes two broad pieces out of his pocket*) See here, they're set in gold.
Gives one to each
APPLETREE
The wonderful works of Nature! *Looking at it*
PEARMAIN
What's this written about? Here's a posy, I believe, *Ca-ro-lus* – what's that, Sergeant?
KITE
Oh, *Carolus*! Why, *Carolus* is Latin for Queen Anne, that's all.
PEARMAIN
'Tis a fine thing to be a scollard – Sergeant, will you part

with this? I'll buy it on you, if it come within the compass of a crawn.

KITE

A crown! Never talk of buying; 'tis the same thing among friends, you know, I present 'em to you both; you shall give me as good a thing. Put 'em up, and remember your old friend, when I'm *over the hills and far away*. *Singing*

They sing and put up the money

Enter PLUME *singing*

PLUME

Over the hills, and o're the main,
To Flanders, Portugal, or Spain;
The Queen commands, and we'll obey,
Over the hills and far away.

Come on my men of mirth, away with it, I'll make one among ye. – Who are these hearty lads?

KITE

Off with your hats; ounds, off with your hats; this is the captain, the captain.

APPLETREE

We have seen captains afore now, mun.

PEARMAIN

Aye, and lieutenant captains too; flesh, I'se keep on my nab.

APPLETREE

And I'se scarcely d'off mine for any captain in England; my vether's a freeholder.

PLUME

Who are these jolly lads, Sergeant?

KITE

A couple of honest, brave fellows that are willing to serve the Queen; I have entertained 'em just now as volunteers under your honour's command.

PLUME

And good entertainment they shall have; volunteers are the men I want, those are the men fit to make soldiers, captains, generals.

PEARMAIN

Wauns, Tummas, what's this? Are you listed?

APPLETREE

Flesh, not I; are you, Costar?

PEARMAIN

Wauns, not I.

KITE

What, not listed! Ha, ha, ha, a very good jest, faith.

PEARMAIN

Come, Tummas, we'll go whome.

APPLETREE

Aye, aye, come.

KITE

Home! For shame, gentlemen, behave yourselves better before your captain – dear Tummas, honest Costar –

PEARMAIN

No, no, we'll be gone. *Going*

KITE

Nay, then I command you to stay: I place you both sentinels in this place for two hours to watch the motion of St Mary's clock, you, and you the motion of St Chad's; and he that dare stir from his post till he be relieved shall have my sword in his guts the next minute.

PLUME

What's the matter, Sergeant? I'm afraid you're too rough with these gentlemen.

KITE

I'm too mild, sir, they disobey command, sir, and one of 'em should be shot for an example to the other.

PEARMAIN

Shot, Tummas!

PLUME

Come, gentlemen, what's the matter?

APPLETREE

We don't know; the noble sergeant is pleased to be in a passion, sir – but –

KITE

They disobey command, they deny their being listed.

PEARMAIN

Nay, Sergeant, we don't downright deny it neither, that we dare not do for fear of being shot; but we humbly conceive in a civil way, and begging your worship's pardon, that we may go home.

PLUME

That's easily known; have either of you received any of the Queen's money?

APPLETREE

Not a brass farthing, sir.

KITE

Sir, they have each of 'em received three and twenty shillings and sixpence, and 'tis now in their pockets.

APPLETREE

Wauns! If I have a penny in my pocket but a bent sixpence, I'll be content to be listed, and shot into the bargain.

PEARMAIN

And I, look'ee here, sir.

APPLETREE

Aye, here's my stock too, nothing but the Queen's picture that the sergeant gave me just now.

KITE

See there, a broad piece, three and twenty shillings and sixpence; the t'other has the fellow on't.

PLUME

The case is plain, gentlemen, the goods are found upon you: those pieces of gold are worth three and twenty and sixpence each.

PEARMAIN

So it seems that *Carolus* is three and twenty shillings and sixpence in Latin.

APPLETREE

'Tis the same thing in the Greek, for we are listed.

PEARMAIN

Flesh, but we an't, Tummas; I desire to be carried before the mayar, Captain.

While they talk, the CAPTAIN *and* SERGEANT *whisper*

PLUME

'Twill never do, Kite; your damned tricks will ruin me at last – I won't lose the fellows though, if I can help it. – Well, gentlemen, there must be some trick in this; my sergeant offers to take his oath that you're fairly listed.

APPLETREE

Why, Captain, we know that you soldiers have more liberty of conscience than other folks, but for me or neighbour Costar here to take such an oath, 'twould be downright perjuration.

PLUME

Look'ee you rascal, you villain, if I find that you have imposed upon these two honest fellows, I'll trample you to death, you dog; come, how was't?

APPLETREE

Nay, then we will speak. Your sergeant, as you say, is a rogue, begging your worship's pardon, and –

PEARMAIN

Nay, Tummas, let me speak, you know I can read. – And so,

sir, he gave us those two pieces of money for pictures of the Queen by way of a present.

PLUME

How! By way of a present! The son of a whore! I'll teach him to abuse honest fellows like you. Scoundrel, rogue, villain, *etc.* *Beats off the* SERGEANT, *and follows*

BOTH

O brave, noble Captain! Huzza! A brave captain, faith.

PEARMAIN

Now, Tummas, *Carolus* is Latin for a beating; this is the bravest captain I ever saw. – Wauns, I have a month's mind to go with him.

Enter PLUME

PLUME

A dog, to abuse two such honest fellows as you! Look'ee, gentlemen, I love a pretty fellow; I come among you here as an officer to list soldiers, not as a kidnapper to steal slaves.

PEARMAIN

Mind that, Tummas.

PLUME

I desire no man to go with me, but as I went myself: I went a volunteer, as you or you may go, for a little time carried a musket, and now I command a company.

APPLETREE

Mind that, Costar, a sweet gentleman.

PLUME

'Tis true, gentlemen, I might take an advantage of you; the Queen's money was in your pockets, my sergeant was ready to take his oath you were listed; but I scorn to do a base thing, you are both of you at your liberty.

PEARMAIN

Thank you, noble Captain. – I cod, I can't find in my heart to leave him, he talks so finely.

APPLETREE

Aye, Costar, would he always hold in this mind?

PLUME

Come, my lads, one thing more I'll tell you: you're both young, tight fellows, and the army is the place to make you men forever: every man has his lot, and you have yours. What think you now of a purse full of French gold out of a monsieur's pocket, after you have dashed out his brains with the butt of your firelock, eh?

PEARMAIN
Wauns, I'll have it, Captain – give me a shilling, I'll follow you to the end of the world.

APPLETREE
Nay, dear Costar, duna; be advised. 160

PLUME
Here, my hero, here are two guineas for thee, as earnest of what I'll do farther for thee.

APPLETREE
Duna take it, duna, dear Costar.
(*Cries, and pulls back his arm*)

PEARMAIN
I wull, I wull – wauns, my mind gives me that I shall be a captain myself. I take your money, sir, and now I'm a 165 gentleman.

PLUME
Give me thy hand. – And now you and I will travel the world o'er, and command wherever we tread. – [*Aside to* PEARMAIN] Bring your friend with you if you can.

PEARMAIN
Well, Tummas, must we part? 170

APPLETREE
No, Costar, I cannot leave thee. Come, Captain (*crying*), I'll e'en go along too, and if you have two honester, simpler lads in your company than we twa been – I'll say no more.

PLUME
Here, my lad. (*Gives him money*) Now your name?

APPLETREE
Thummas Appletree. 175

PLUME
And yours?

PEARMAIN
Costar Pearmain.

PLUME
Born where?

APPLETREE
Both in Herefordshire.

PLUME
Very well. Courage, my lads, now we'll sing *Over the hills* 180 *and far away*.

Courage, boys, 'tis one to ten,
But we return all gentlemen;
While conquering colours we display,

Over the hills and far away. 185
Over, &c. *Exeunt*

Act III, Scene i

The Market-place
Enter PLUME *and* WORTHY

WORTHY
I can't forbear admiring the equality of our two fortunes: we loved two ladies, they met us halfway, and just as we were upon the point of leaping into their arms, fortune drops into their laps, pride possesses their hearts, a maggot fills their heads, madness takes 'em by the tails, they snort, kick up their 5 heels, and away they run.

PLUME
And leave us here to mourn upon the shore – a couple of poor, melancholy monsters – what shall we do?

WORTHY
I have a trick for mine; the letter, you know, and the fortune-teller. 10

PLUME
And I have a trick for mine.

WORTHY
What is't?

PLUME
I'll never think of her again.

WORTHY
No!

PLUME
No; I think myself above administering to the pride of any 15 woman, were she worth twelve thousand a year, and I han't the vanity to believe I shall ever gain a lady worth twelve hundred; the generous, good-natured Silvia in her smock I admire, but the haughty, scornful Silvia, with her fortune, I despise. 20

A SONG

1

Come, fair one, be kind,
You never shall find
A fellow so fit for a lover;
The world shall view

My passion for you,
But never your passion discover.

2

I still will complain
Of your frowns and disdain,
Though I revel through all your charms;
The world shall declare,
That I die with despair,
When I only die in your arms.

3

I still will adore,
And love more and more,
But, by Jove, if you chance to prove cruel:
I'll get me a miss
That freely will kiss,
Though I afterwards drink water-gruel.

What, sneak out o'town and not so much as a word, a line, a compliment – 'sdeath! How far off does she live? I'll go and break her windows.

WORTHY

Ha, ha, ha; aye, and the window bars too to come at her. Come, come, friend, no more of your rough, military airs.

Enter KITE

KITE

Captain, sir, look yonder, she's a-coming this way, 'tis the prettiest, cleanest, little tit.

PLUME

Now, Worthy, to show you how much I'm in love – here she comes, and what is that great country fellow with her?

KITE

I can't tell, sir.

Enter ROSE *and her brother* BULLOCK, ROSE *with a basket on her arm, crying 'Chickens'*

ROSE

Buy chickens, young and tender, young and tender chickens.

PLUME

Here, you chickens!

ROSE

Who calls?

PLUME
Come hither, pretty maid.
ROSE
Will you please to buy, sir?
WORTHY
Yes, child, we'll both buy.
PLUME
Nay, Worthy, that's not fair, market for yourself; come, child, I'll buy all you have.
ROSE
Then all I have is at your sarvice. *Curtsies*
WORTHY
Then I must shift for myself, I find. *Exit*
PLUME
Let me see – young and tender, you say?
Chucks her under the chin
ROSE
As ever you tasted in your life, sir. *Curtsies*
PLUME
Come, I must examine your basket to the bottom, my dear.
ROSE
Nay, for that matter, put in your hand; feel, sir; I warrant my ware as good as any in the market.
PLUME
And I'll buy it all, child, were it ten times more.
ROSE
Sir, I can furnish you.
PLUME
Come then; we won't quarrel about the price, they're fine birds; pray what's your name, pretty creature?
ROSE
Rose, sir; my father is a farmer within three short mile o'th' town; we keep this market; I sell chickens, eggs, and butter, and my brother Bullock there sells corn.
BULLOCK
Come, sister, haste ye; we shall be liate a whome.

All this while BULLOCK *whistles about the stage*

PLUME
Kite! (*Tips him the wink, he returns it*) Pretty Mrs Rose – you have – let me see – how many?
ROSE
A dozen, sir, and they are richly worth a crawn.

BULLOCK

Come, Ruose, Ruose, I sold fifty stracke o'barley today in half this time; but you will higgle and higgle for a penny more than the commodity is worth.

ROSE

What's that to you, oaf? I can make as much out of a groat as you can out of fourpence, I'm sure – the gentleman bids fair, and when I meet with a chapman, I know how to make the best on him – and so, sir, I say for a crawn piece the bargain's yours.

PLUME

Here's a guinea, my dear.

ROSE

I con't change your money, sir.

PLUME

Indeed, indeed but you can – my lodging is hard by, chicken, and we'll make change there. *Goes off, she follows him*

KITE

So, sir, as I was telling you, I have seen one of these hussars eat up a ravelin for his breakfast and afterwards pick his teeth with a palisado.

BULLOCK

Aye, you soldiers see very strange things – but pray, sir, what is a ravelin?

KITE

Why 'tis like a modern minced pie, but the crust is confounded hard, and the plums are somewhat hard of digestion!

BULLOCK

Then your palisado, pray what may he be? – Come, Ruose, pray ha' done.

KITE

Your palisado is a pretty sort of bodkin about the thickness of my leg.

BULLOCK

(*Aside*) – That's a fib, I believe. – Eh, where's Ruose? Ruose! Ruose! 'sflesh, where's Ruose gone?

KITE

She's gone with the captain.

BULLOCK

The captain! Wauns, there's no pressing of women, sure?

KITE

But there is, sir.

BULLOCK

If the captain should press Ruose, I should be ruined; which way went she? – Oh, the devil take your rablins and palisaders. *Exit*

KITE

You shall be better acquainted with them, honest Bullock, or I shall miss of my aim.

Enter WORTHY

WORTHY

Why, thou'rt the most useful fellow in nature to your captain, admirable in your way, I find.

KITE

Yes, sir, I understand my business, I will say it; you must know, sir, I was born a gypsy, and bred among that crew till I was ten year old, there I learned canting and lying; I was bought from my mother Cleopatra by a certain nobleman for three pistoles, who liking my beauty made me his page, there I learned impudence and pimping; I was turned off for wearing my lord's linen, and drinking my lady's ratafia; and then turned bailiff's follower, there I learned bullying and swearing. I at last got into the army, and there I learned whoring and drinking. – So that if your worship pleases to cast up the whole sum, viz., canting, lying, impudence, pimping, bullying, swearing, whoring, drinking, and a halberd, you will find the sum total will amount to a recruiting sergeant.

WORTHY

And pray, what induced you to turn soldier?

KITE

Hunger and ambition – the fears of starving and hopes of a truncheon led me along to a gentleman with a fair tongue and fair periwig, who loaded me with promises; but I gad 'twas the lightest load that I ever felt in my life – he promised to advance me, and indeed he did so – to a garret in the Savoy. I asked him why he put me in prison; he called me lying dog, and said I was in garrison; and indeed 'tis a garrison that may hold out till doomsday before I should desire to take it again. But here comes Justice Balance.

Enter BALANCE *and* BULLOCK

BALANCE

Here, you Sergeant, where's your captain? Here's a poor, foolish fellow comes clamouring to me with a complaint, that your captain has pressed his sister; do you know anything of this matter, Worthy?

WORTHY

Ha, ha, ha, I know his sister is gone with Plume to his lodgings to sell him some chickens. 140

BALANCE

Is that all? The fellow's a fool.

BULLOCK

I know that, an't please you; but if your worship pleases to grant me a warrant to bring her before you for fear o' th' worst.

BALANCE

Thou'rt mad, fellow, thy sister's safe enough. 145

KITE (*Aside*)

I hope so too.

WORTHY

Hast thou no more sense, fellow, than to believe that the captain can list women?

BULLOCK

I know not whether they list them, or what they do with them, but I'm sure they carry as many women as men with 150 them out of the country.

BALANCE

But how came you not to go along with your sister?

BULLOCK

Luord, sir, I thought no more of her going than I do of the day I shall die; but this gentleman here, not suspecting any hurt neither, I believe – you thought no harm, friend, did ye? 155

KITE

Lack-a-day, sir, not I. – (*Aside*) Only that I believe I shall marry her tomorrow.

BALANCE

I begin to smell powder. Well, friend, but what did that gentleman with you?

BULLOCK

Why, sir, he entertained me with a fine story of a great fight 160 between the Hungarians, I think it was, and the Irish.

KITE

And so, sir, while we were in the heat of the battle, the captain carried off the baggage.

BALANCE

Sergeant, go along with this fellow to your captain, give him my humble service, and desire him to discharge the wench, 165 though he has listed her.

BULLOCK

Aye – and if he ben't free for that, he shall have another man in her place.

KITE

Come, honest friend. – (*Aside*) You shall go to my quarters instead of the captain's. *Exeunt* KITE *and* BULLOCK 170

BALANCE

We must get this mad captain his complement of men, and send him a-packing, else he'll overrun the country.

WORTHY

You see, sir, how little he values your daughter's disdain.

BALANCE

I like him the better; I was much such another fellow at his age; I never set my heart upon any woman so much as to 175 make me uneasy at the disappointment; but what was very surprising both to myself and friends, I changed o' th' sudden from the most fickle lover to the most constant husband in the world. But how goes your affair with Melinda?

WORTHY

Very slowly. Cupid had formerly wings, but I think in this 180 age he goes upon crutches, or I fancy Venus had been dallying with her cripple Vulcan when my amour commenced, which has made it go on so lamely. My mistress has got a captain too, but such a captain! As I live, yonder he comes. 185

BALANCE

Who? That bluff fellow in the sash? I don't know him.

WORTHY

But I engage he knows you, and everybody at first sight; his impudence were a prodigy, were not his ignorance proportionable; he has the most universal acquaintance of any man living, for he won't be alone, and nobody will keep him 190 company twice; then he's a Caesar among the women, *veni, vidi, vici*, that's all. If he has but talked with the maid, he swears he has lain with the mistress; but the most surprising part of his character is his memory, which is the most prodigious, and the most trifling in the world. 195

BALANCE

I have met with such men, and I take this good-for-nothing memory to proceed from a certain contexture of the brain, which is purely adapted to impertinencies, and there they lodge secure, the owner having no thoughts of his own to disturb them. I have known a man as perfect as a chronologer 200 as to the day and year of most important transactions, but be altogether ignorant of the causes, springs, or consequences of any one thing of moment; I have known another acquire so much by travel, as to tell you the names of most places in Europe, with their distances of miles, leagues, or hours, as punctually as a post-boy; but for anything else, as ignorant as the horse that carries the mail.

WORTHY

This is your man, sir, add but the traveller's privilege of lying, and even that he abuses; this is the picture, behold the life.

Enter BRAZEN

BRAZEN

Mr Worthy, I'm your servant, and so forth – hark'ee, my dear –

WORTHY

Whispering, sir, before company is not manners, and when nobody's by, 'tis foolish.

BRAZEN

Company! *Mort de ma vie*, I beg the gentleman's pardon, who is he?

WORTHY

Ask him.

BRAZEN

So I will. – My dear, I'm your servant, and so forth, – your name, my dear?

BALANCE

Very laconic, sir.

BRAZEN

Laconic, a very good name truly; I have known several of the Laconics abroad. Poor Jack Laconic! He was killed at the battle of Landen. I remember that he had a blue ribband in his hat that very day, and after he fell, we found a piece of neat's tongue in his pocket.

BALANCE

Pray, sir, did the French attack us or we them at Landen?

BRAZEN

The French attack us! Oons, sir, are you a Jacobite?

BALANCE

Why that question?

BRAZEN

Because none but a Jacobite could think that the French durst attack us – no, sir, we attacked them on the – I have reason to remember the time, for I had two-and-twenty horses killed under me that day.

WORTHY

Then, sir, you must have rid mighty hard.

BALANCE

Or perhaps, sir, like my countryman, you rid upon half a dozen horses at once.

BRAZEN

What d'e mean, gentlemen? I tell you they were killed, all torn to pieces by cannon-shot, except six that I staked to death upon the enemy's *chevaux de frise.*

BALANCE

Noble Captain, may I crave your name?

BRAZEN

Brazen, at your service.

BALANCE

Oh, Brazen, a very good name, I have known several of the Brazens abroad.

WORTHY

Do you know Captain Plume, sir?

BRAZEN

Is he anything related to Frank Plume in Northamptonshire? – Honest Frank! Many, many a dry bottle have we cracked hand to fist; you must have known his brother Charles that was concerned in the India Company, he married the daughter of old Tongue-Pad, the Master in Chancery, a very pretty woman, only squinted a little; she died in childbed of her first child, but the child survived, 'twas a daughter, but whether 'twas called Margaret or Marjory, upon my soul I can't remember – but, gentlemen (*looking on his watch*), I must meet a lady, a twenty-thousand-pounder, presently, upon the walk by the water – Worthy, your servant; Laconic, yours. *Exit*

BALANCE

If you can have so mean an opinion of Melinda, as to be jealous of this fellow, I think she ought to give you cause to be so.

WORTHY

I don't think she encourages him so much for gaining herself a lover, as to set me up a rival; were there any credit to be given to his words, I should believe Melinda had made him this assignation; I must go see – sir, you'll pardon me.

BALANCE

Aye, aye, sir, you're a man of business. [*Exit* WORTHY]
But what have we got here?

Enter ROSE *singing*

ROSE

And I shall be a lady, a captain's lady, and ride single upon a white horse with a star, upon a velvet sidesaddle; and I shall go to London and see the tombs and the lions, and the Queen. Sir, an't please your worship, I have often seen your worship ride through our grounds a-hunting, begging your worship's pardon – pray, what may this lace be worth a yard? *Showing some lace*

BALANCE

Right Mechlin, by this light! Where did you get this lace, child?

ROSE

No matter for that, sir, I come honestly by't.

BALANCE

I question it much.

ROSE

And see here, sir, a fine turkey-shell snuff-box, and fine mangeree, see here: (*takes snuff affectedly*) the captain learnt me how to take it with an air.

BALANCE

Oho, the captain! Now the murder's out – and so the captain taught you to take it with an air?

ROSE

Yes, and give it with an air too – will your worship please to taste my snuff? *Offers the box affectedly*

BALANCE

You're a very apt scholar, pretty maid. And pray what did you give the captain for these fine things?

ROSE

He's to have my brother for a soldier, and two or three sweethearts that I have in the country, they shall all go with the captain. Oh, he's the finest man, and the humblest withal; would you believe it, sir, he carried me up with him to his own chamber with as much familiarity as if I had been the best lady in the land.

BALANCE

Oh, he's a mighty familiar gentleman as can be.

Enter PLUME *singing*

PLUME

But it is not so
With those that go

Through frost and snow
Most apropos,
My maid with the milking-pail. 295
Takes hold on ROSE
How, the justice! Then I'm arraigned, condemned, and executed.

BALANCE
Oh, my noble Captain.

ROSE
And my noble captain too, sir.

PLUME
'Sdeath, child, are you mad? – Mr Balance, I am so full of 300 business about my recruits, that I han't a moment's time to – I have just now three or four people to –

BALANCE
Nay, Captain, I must speak to you.

ROSE
And so must I too, Captain.

PLUME
Any other time, sir – I cannot for my life, sir – 305

BALANCE
Pray, sir.

PLUME
Twenty thousand things – I would but – now, sir, pray – devil take me – I cannot – I must – *Breaks away*

BALANCE
Nay, I'll follow you. *Exit*

ROSE
And I too. *Exit* 310

[Act III], Scene ii

The Walk by the Severn side
Enter MELINDA *and her maid* LUCY

MELINDA
And pray, was it a ring, or buckle, or pendants, or knots; or in what shape was the almighty gold transformed that has bribed you so much in his favour?

LUCY
Indeed, madam, the last bribe I had was from the captain, and that was only a small piece of Flanders edging for 5 pinners.

MELINDA

Aye, Flanders lace is as constant a present from officers to their women as something else is from their women to them. They every year bring over a cargo of lace to cheat the Queen of her duty, and her subjects of their honesty.

LUCY

They only barter one sort of prohibited goods for another, madam.

MELINDA

Has any of them been bartering with you, Mrs Pert, that you talk so like a trader?

LUCY

Madam, you talk as peevishly to me as if it were my fault, the crime is none of mine though I pretend to excuse it; though he should not see you this week, can I help it? But as I was saying, madam, his friend Captain Plume has so taken him up these two days –

MELINDA

Psha! Would his friend, the captain, were tied upon his back; I warrant he has never been sober since that confounded captain came to town; the devil take all officers, I say – they do the nation more harm by debauching us at home, than they do good by defending us abroad: no sooner a captain comes to town, but all the young fellows flock about him, and we can't keep a man to ourselves.

LUCY

One would imagine, madam, by your concern for Worthy's absence, that you should use him better when he's with you.

MELINDA

Who told you, pray, that I was concerned for his absence? I'm only vexed that I've had nothing said to me these two days: one may like the love and despise the lover, I hope; as one may love the treason and hate the traitor. Oh! Here comes another captain, and a rogue that has the confidence to make love to me; but indeed I don't wonder at that, when he has the assurance to fancy himself a fine gentleman.

LUCY (*Aside*)

If he should speak o' th' assignation, I should be ruined.

Enter BRAZEN

BRAZEN

True to the touch, faith. (*Aside*) I'll draw up all my compliments into one grand platoon, and fire upon her at once.

Thou peerless princess of Salopian plains,
Envied by nymphs and worshipped by the swains,
Behold how humbly does the Severn glide,
To greet thee, princess of the Severn side.

Madam, I'm your humble servant and all that, madam – a fine river this same Severn – do you love fishing, madam?

MELINDA

'Tis a pretty melancholy amusement for lovers.

BRAZEN

I'll go buy hooks and lines presently; for you must know, madam, that I have served in Flanders against the French, in Hungary against the Turks, and in Tangier against the Moors, and I was never so much in love before; and split me, madam, in all the campaigns I ever made I have not seen so fine a woman as your ladyship.

MELINDA

And from all the men I ever saw I never had so fine a compliment; but you soldiers are the best-bred men, that we must allow.

BRAZEN

Some of us, madam, but there are brutes among us too, very sad brutes; for my own part, I have always had the good luck to prove agreeable – I have had very considerable offers, madam, I might have married a German princess worth fifty thousand crowns a year, but her stove disgusted me. The daughter of a Turkish bashaw fell in love with me too when I was prisoner among the infidels; she offered to rob her father of his treasure, and make her escape with me, but I don't know how, my time was not come; hanging and marriage, you know, go by destiny; Fate has reserved me for a Shropshire lady with twenty thousand pound – do you know any such person, madam?

MELINDA

Extravagant coxcomb! – To be sure, a great many ladies of that fortune would be proud of the name of Mrs Brazen.

BRAZEN

Nay, for that matter, madam, there are women of very good quality of the name of Brazen.

Enter WORTHY

MELINDA

Oh, are you there, gentleman? – Come, Captain, we'll walk this way, give me your hand.

BRAZEN

My hand, heart's blood, and guts are at your service. –
Mr Worthy – your servant, my dear. *Exit leading* MELINDA

WORTHY

Death and fire! This is not to be borne. 75

Enter PLUME

PLUME

No more it is, faith.

WORTHY

What?

PLUME

The March beer at the Raven; I have been doubly serving the Queen, – raising men and raising the excise – recruiting and elections are rare friends to the excise. 80

WORTHY

You an't drunk?

PLUME

No, no, whimsical only; I could be mighty foolish, and fancy myself mighty witty; Reason still keeps its throne, but it nods a little, that's all.

WORTHY

Then you're just fit for a frolic? 85

PLUME

As fit as close pinners for a punk in the pit.

WORTHY

There's your play then, recover me that vessel from that Tangerine.

PLUME

She's well rigged, but how is she manned?

WORTHY

By Captain Brazen that I told you of today; she is called 90
the Melinda, a first rate I can assure you; she sheered off with him just now on purpose to affront me, but according to your advice I would take no notice, because I would seem to be above a concern for her behaviour. But have a care of a quarrel. 95

PLUME

No, no, I never quarrel with anything in my cups but an oyster wench or a cook maid, and if they ben't civil, I knock 'em down. But hark'ee my friend, I will make love, and I must make love. I tell'ee what, I'll make love like a platoon.

WORTHY

Platoon, how's that? 100

PLUME
I'll kneel, stoop, and stand, faith; most ladies are gained by platooning.

WORTHY
Here they come; I must leave you. *Exit*

PLUME
So – now must I look as sober and demure as a whore at a christening. 105

Enter BRAZEN *and* MELINDA

BRAZEN
Who's that, madam?

MELINDA
A brother officer of yours, I suppose, sir.

BRAZEN
Aye! – (*To* PLUME) My dear.

PLUME
My dear! *They run and embrace*

BRAZEN
My dear boy, how is't? – Your name, my dear? If I be not 110
mistaken, I have seen your face.

PLUME
I never see yours in my life, my dear – but there's a face well known as the sun's, that shines on all and is by all adored.

BRAZEN
Have you any pretensions, sir? 115

PLUME
Pretensions!

BRAZEN
That is, sir, have you ever served abroad?

PLUME
I have served at home, sir, for ages served this cruel fair – and that will serve the turn, sir.

MELINDA (*Aside*)
So, between the fool and the rake I shall bring a fine spot of 120
work upon my hands – I see Worthy yonder, I could be content to be friends with him would he come this way.

BRAZEN
Will you fight for the lady, sir?

PLUME
No, sir, but I'll have her notwithstanding.
Thou peerless princess of Salopian plains, 125
Envied by nymphs and worshipped by the swains—

BRAZEN
Oons, sir, not fight for her!

PLUME
Prithee be quiet, I shall be out –
Behold how humbly does the Severn glide
To greet thee, princess of the Severn side. 130

BRAZEN
Don't mind him, madam. – If he were not so well dressed I should take him for a poet; but I'll show the difference presently – come, madam, we'll place you between us, and now the longest sword carries her.

Draws, MELINDA *shrieks*

Enter WORTHY

MELINDA
Oh, Mr Worthy, save me from these madmen. 135

Runs off with WORTHY

PLUME
Ha, ha, ha, why don't you follow, sir, and fight the bold ravisher?

BRAZEN
No, sir, you're my man.

PLUME
I don't like the wages, and I won't be your man.

BRAZEN
Then you're not worth my sword. 140

PLUME
No? Pray what did it cost?

BRAZEN
It cost me twenty pistoles in France, and my enemies thousands of lives in Flanders.

PLUME
Then they had a dear bargain.

Enter SILVIA *dressed in man's apparel*

SILVIA
Save ye, save ye, gentlemen. 145

BRAZEN
My dear, I'm yours.

PLUME
Do you know the gentleman?

BRAZEN
No, but I will presently. – Your name, my dear?

SILVIA
Wilful, Jack Wilful, at your service.
BRAZEN
What! The Kentish Wilfuls or those of Staffordshire?
SILVIA
Both, sir, both; I'm related to all the Wilfuls in Europe, and I'm head of the family at present.
PLUME
Do you live in this country, sir?
SILVIA
Yes, sir, I live where I stand, I have neither home, house, nor habitation beyond this spot of ground.
BRAZEN
What are you, sir?
SILVIA
A rake.
PLUME
In the army, I presume.
SILVIA
No, but intend to list immediately – look'ee, gentlemen, he that bids me fairest has me.
BRAZEN
Sir, I'll prefer you, I'll make you a corporal this minute.
PLUME
A corporal! I'll make you my companion, you shall eat with me.
BRAZEN
You shall drink with me.
PLUME
You shall lie with me, you young rogue. *Kisses her*
BRAZEN
You shall receive your pay and do no duty.
SILVIA
Then you must make me a field-officer.
PLUME
Pho, pho, I'll do more than all this, I'll make you a corporal, and give you a brevet for sergeant.
BRAZEN
Can you read and write, sir?
SILVIA
Yes.
BRAZEN
Then your business is done, I'll make you chaplain to the regiment.

SILVIA

Your promises are so equal that I'm at a loss to choose; there is one Plume that I hear much commended in town, pray which of you is Captain Plume?

PLUME

I am Captain Plume.

BRAZEN

No, no, I'm Captain Plume.

SILVIA

Hey day!

PLUME

Captain Plume, I'm your servant, my dear.

BRAZEN

Captain Brazen, I'm yours. – The fellow dare not fight.

Enter KITE

KITE

Sir, if you please – *Goes to whisper* PLUME

PLUME

No, no, there's your captain. – Captain Plume, your sergeant here has got so drunk he mistakes me for you.

BRAZEN

He's an incorrigible sot. – Here, my Hector of Holborn, forty shillings for you.

PLUME

I forbid the banns – look'ee, friend, you shall list with Captain Brazen.

SILVIA

I will see Captain Brazen hanged first, I will list with Captain Plume; I'm a freeborn Englishman and will be a slave my own way. – (*To* BRAZEN) Look'ee, sir, will you stand by me?

BRAZEN

I warrant you, my lad.

SILVIA

Then I will tell you, Captain Brazen (*to* PLUME), that you are an ignorant, pretending, impudent coxcomb.

BRAZEN

Aye, aye, a sad dog.

SILVIA

A very sad dog; give me the money, noble Captain Plume.

PLUME

Then you won't list with Captain Brazen?

SILVIA
I won't.

BRAZEN
Never mind him, child, I'll end the dispute presently; hark'ee, my dear –

Takes PLUME *to one side of the stage and entertains him in dumb show*

KITE
Sir, he in the plain coat is Captain Plume; I'm his sergeant and will take my oath on't.

SILVIA
What! You are Sergeant Kite?

KITE
At your service.

SILVIA
Then I would not take your oath for a farthing.

KITE
A very understanding youth of his age. Pray, sir, let me look you full in the face.

SILVIA
Well, sir, what have you to say to my face?

KITE
The very image and superscription of my brother, two bullets of the same calibre were never so like; sure it must be Charles, Charles –

SILVIA
What d'ye mean by Charles?

KITE
The voice too, only a little variation in effa ut flat; my dear brother, for I must call you so, if you should have the fortune to enter into the most noble society of the sword, I bespeak you for a comrade.

SILVIA
No, sir, I'll be your captain's comrade if anybody's.

KITE
Ambition! There again, 'tis a noble passion for a soldier; by that I gained this glorious halberd. Ambition! I see a commission in his face already; pray, noble Captain, give me leave to salute you. *Offers to kiss her*

SILVIA
What, men kiss one another!

KITE
We officers do, 'tis our way; we live together like man and

wife, always either kissing or fighting. – But I see a storm a-coming. 225

SILVIA

Now, Sergeant, I shall see who is your captain by your knocking down the t'other.

KITE

My captain scorns assistance, sir.

BRAZEN

How dare you contend for anything and not dare to draw your sword? But you're a young fellow, and have not been much abroad, I excuse that; but prithee resign the man, prithee do; you're a very honest fellow. 230

PLUME

You lie, and you're a son of a whore.

Draws, and makes up to BRAZEN

BRAZEN (*Retiring*)

Hold, hold, did not you refuse to fight for the lady? 235

PLUME

I always do – but for a man I'll fight knee deep, so you lie again.

PLUME *and* BRAZEN *fight a traverse or two about the stage;* SILVIA *draws, and is held by* KITE, *who sounds to arms with his mouth, takes* SILVIA *in his arms, and carries her off the stage*

BRAZEN

Hold – where's the man?

PLUME

Gone.

BRAZEN

Then what do we fight for? (*Puts up*) Now let's embrace, my dear. 240

PLUME

With all my heart, my dear. (*Putting up*) I suppose Kite has listed him by this time. *They embrace*

BRAZEN

You're a brave fellow. I always fight with a man before I make him my friend; and if once I find he will fight, I never quarrel with him afterwards. – And now I'll tell you a secret, my dear friend, that lady we frighted out o'the walk just now I found in bed this morning, so beautiful, so inviting – I presently locked the door – but I'm a man of honour – but I believe I shall marry her nevertheless; her twenty thousand pound, you know, will be a pretty conveniency – I had an assignation with her here, but your 245 250 coming spoiled my sport, curse ye, my dear, – but don't do so again.

PLUME

No, no, my dear, men are my business at present. 255

Exeunt

Act IV, Scene i

The Walk by the Severn side
[*Enter*] ROSE *and* BULLOCK *meeting*

ROSE

Where have you been, you great booby? You're always out o' th'way in the time of preferment.

BULLOCK

Preferment! Who should prefer me?

ROSE

I would prefer you; who should prefer a man but a woman? Come throw away that great club, hold up your head, 5 cock your hat, and look big.

BULLOCK

Ah! Ruose, Ruose, I fear somebody will look big sooner than folk think of; this genteel breeding never comes into the country without a train of followers. – Here has been Cartwheel your sweetheart, what will become o' him? 10

ROSE

Look'ee, I'm a great woman and will provide for my relations; I told the captain how finely he played upon the tabor and pipe, so he has set him down for drum-major.

BULLOCK

Nay, sister, why did not you keep that place for me? You know I always loved to be a-drumming, if it were but on a 15 table, or on a quart pot.

Enter SILVIA

SILVIA

Had I but a commission in my pocket I fancy my breeches would become me as well as any ranting fellow of 'em all; for I take a bold step, a rakish toss, a smart cock, and an impudent air to be the principal ingredients in the com- 20 position of a captain. – What's here? Rose, my nurse's daughter. I'll go and practise. – Come, child, kiss me at once. (*Kisses* ROSE) And her brother too. – Well, honest Dungfork, do you know the difference between a horse cart and a cart horse, eh? 25

BULLOCK

I presume that your worship is a captain by your clothes and your courage.

SILVIA

Suppose I were, would you be contented to list, friend?

ROSE

No, no, though your worship be a handsome man, there be others as fine as you; my brother is engaged to Captain Plume.

SILVIA

Plume! Do you know Captain Plume?

ROSE

Yes, I do, and he knows me. – He took the very ribbands out of his shirtsleeves and put 'em into my shoes – see there. – I can assure you that I can do anything with the captain.

BULLOCK

That is, in a modest way, sir. – Have a care what you say, Ruose, don't shame your parentage.

ROSE

Nay, for that matter I am not so simple as to say that I can do anything with the captain, but what I may do with anybody else.

SILVIA

So! And pray what do you expect from this captain, child?

ROSE

I expect, sir! I expect – but he ordered me to tell nobody – but suppose that he should promise to marry me?

SILVIA

You should have a care, my dear, men will promise anything beforehand.

ROSE

I know that, but he promised to marry me afterwards.

BULLOCK

Wauns, Ruose, what have you said?

SILVIA

Afterwards! After what?

ROSE

After I had sold him my chickens. – I hope there's no harm in that.

Enter PLUME

PLUME

What, Mr Wilful, so close with my market-woman!

SILVIA

(*Aside*) I'll try if he loves her. – Close, sir! aye, and closer yet, sir. – Come, my pretty maid, you and I will withdraw a little.

PLUME

No, no, friend, I han't done with her yet.

SILVIA

Nor have I begun with her, so I have as good a right as you have.

PLUME

Thou art a bloody impudent fellow.

SILVIA

Sir, I would qualify myself for the service.

PLUME

Hast thou really a mind to the service?

SILVIA

Yes, sir; so let her go.

ROSE

Pray, gentlemen, don't be so violent.

PLUME

Come, leave it to the girl's own choice. – Will you belong to me or to that gentleman?

ROSE

Let me consider, you're both very handsome.

PLUME

Now the natural inconstancy of her sex begins to work.

ROSE

Pray, sir, what will you give me?

BULLOCK

Dunna be angry, sir, that my sister should be mercenary, for she's but young.

SILVIA

Give thee, child! – I'll set thee above scandal; you shall have a coach with six before and six behind, an equipage to make vice fashionable, and put virtue out of countenance.

PLUME

Pho, that's easily done, – I'll do more for thee, child, I'll buy you a furbelow scarf, and give you a ticket to see a play.

BULLOCK

A play! Wauns, Ruose, take the ticket, and let's see the show.

SILVIA

Look'ee, Captain, if you won't resign, I'll go list with Captain Brazen this minute.

PLUME

Will you list with me if I give up my title?

SILVIA

I will.

PLUME

Take her: I'll change a woman for a man at any time.

ROSE

I have heard before, indeed, that you captains used to sell your men.

BULLOCK

(*Crying*) Pray, Captain, don't send Ruose to the West Indies.

PLUME

Ha, ha, ha, West Indies! No, no, my honest lad, give me thy hand; nor you nor she shall move a step farther than I do. – This gentleman is one of us, and will be kind to you, Mrs Rose.

ROSE

But will you be so kind to me, sir, as the captain would?

SILVIA

I can't be altogether so kind to you, my circumstances are not so good as the captain's; but I'll take care of you, upon my word.

PLUME

Aye, aye, we'll all take care of her; she shall live like a princess, and her brother here shall be – what would you be?

BULLOCK

Ah! sir, if you had not promised the place of drum-major –

PLUME

Aye, that is promised – but what think ye of barrack-master? You're a person of understanding, and barrack-master you shall be. – But what's become of this same Cartwheel you told me of, my dear?

ROSE

We'll go fetch him – come, brother barrack-master. – We shall find you at home, noble Captain?

Exeunt ROSE *and* BULLOCK

PLUME

Yes, yes – and now, sir, here are your forty shillings.

SILVIA

Captain Plume, I despise your listing-money; if I do serve, 'tis purely for love – of that wench I mean. For you must know, that among my other sallies, I have spent the best part of my fortune in search of a maid, and could never find one hitherto; so you may be assured I'd not sell my freedom under a less purchase than I did my estate. – So before I list I must be certified that this girl is a virgin.

PLUME

Mr Wilful, I can't tell how you can be certified in that point, till you try, but upon my honour she may be a vestal for aught that I know to the contrary. – I gained her heart indeed by some trifling presents and promises, and knowing that the best security for a woman's soul is her body, I would have made myself master of that too, had not the jealousy of my impertinent landlady interposed.

SILVIA

So you only want an opportunity for accomplishing your designs upon her?

PLUME

Not at all, I have already gained my ends, which were only the drawing in one or two of her followers. The women, you know, are the loadstones everywhere: gain the wives and you're caressed by the husbands; please the mistresses and you are valued by their gallants; secure an interest with the finest women at court and you procure the favour of the greatest men; so, kiss the prettiest country wenches and you are sure of listing the lustiest fellows. Some people may call this artifice, but I term it stratagem, since it is so main a part of the service – besides, the fatigue of recruiting is so intolerable, that unless we could make ourselves some pleasure amidst the pain, no mortal man would be able to bear it.

SILVIA

Well, sir, I'm satisfied as to the point in debate; but now let me beg you to lay aside your recruiting airs, put on the man of honour, and tell me plainly what usage I must expect when I'm under your command.

PLUME

You must know in the first place, then, that I hate to have gentlemen in my company, for they are always troublesome and expensive, sometimes dangerous; and 'tis a constant maxim amongst us, that those who know the least obey the best. Notwithstanding all this, I find something so agreeable about you, that engages me to court your company; and I can't tell how it is, but I should be uneasy to see you under the command of anybody else. – Your usage will chiefly depend upon your behaviour; only this you must expect, that if you commit a small fault I will excuse it, if a great one, I'll discharge you; for something tells me I shall not be able to punish you.

SILVIA

And something tells me, that if you do discharge me 'twill be the greatest punishment you can inflict; for were we this moment to go upon the greatest dangers in your profession, they would be less terrible to me than to stay behind you. – And now your hand, – this lists me – and now you are my captain.

PLUME

Your friend. (*Kisses her*) 'Sdeath! There's something in this fellow that charms me.

SILVIA

One favour I must beg – this affair will make some noise, and I have some friends that would censure my conduct if I threw myself into the circumstance of a private sentinel of my own head; I must therefore take care to be impressed by the Act of Parliament; you shall leave that to me.

PLUME

What you please as to that. – Will you lodge at my quarters in the meantime? You shall have part of my bed.

SILVIA

Oh, fie, lie with a common soldier! – Would not you rather lie with a common woman?

PLUME

No, faith, I'm not that rake that the world imagines; I have got an air of freedom which people mistake for lewdness in me, as they mistake formality in others for religion; the world is all a cheat, only I take mine which is undesigned to be more excusable than theirs, which is hypocritical; I hurt nobody but myself, and they abuse all mankind. – Will you lie with me?

SILVIA

No, no, Captain, you forget Rose, she's to be my bedfellow you know.

PLUME

I had forgot, pray be kind to her. *Exeunt severally*

Enter MELINDA *and* LUCY

MELINDA

'Tis the greatest misfortune in nature for a woman to want a confidante: we are so weak that we can do nothing without assistance, and then a secret racks us worse than the colic; I'm at this minute so sick of a secret that I'm ready to faint away – help me, Lucy.

LUCY

Bless me, madam, what's the matter?

MELINDA

Vapours only – I begin to recover – if Silvia were in town, I could heartily forgive her faults for the ease of discovering my own.

LUCY

You're thoughtful, madam; am not I worthy to know the cause?

MELINDA

You're a servant, and a secret would make you saucy.

LUCY

Not unless you should find fault without a cause, madam.

MELINDA

Cause or no cause, I must not lose the pleasure of chiding when I please; women must discharge their vapours somewhere, and before we get husbands, our servants must expect to bear with 'em.

LUCY

Then, madam, you had better raise me to a degree above a servant: you know my family, and that five hundred pound would set me upon the foot of a gentlewoman, and make me worthy the confidence of any lady in the land. Besides, madam, 'twill extremely encourage me in the great design I now have in hand.

MELINDA

I don't find that your design can be of any great advantage to you; 'twill please me indeed in the humour I have of being revenged on the fool for his vanity of making love to me, so I don't much care if I do promise you five hundred pound upon my day of marriage.

LUCY

That is the way, madam, to make me diligent in the vocation of a confidante, which I think is generally to bring people together.

MELINDA

Oh, Lucy, I can hold my secret no longer – you must know that hearing of the famous fortune-teller in town, I went disguised to satisfy a curiosity which has cost me dear; that fellow is certainly the devil, or one of his bosom favourites, he has told me the most surprising things of my past life –

LUCY

Things past, madam, can hardly be reckoned surprising,

because we know them already; did he tell you anything surprising that was to come?

MELINDA

One thing very surprising, he said I should die a maid.

LUCY

Die a maid! Come into the world for nothing! – Dear madam, if you should believe him, it might come to pass; for the bare thought on't might kill one in four and twenty hours. – And did you ask him any questions about me?

MELINDA

You! Why, I passed for you.

LUCY

So 'tis I that am to die a maid – but the devil was a liar from the beginning, he can't make me die a maid – I have put it out of his power already.

MELINDA

I do but jest, I would have passed for you, and called myself Lucy, but he presently told me my name, my quality, my fortune, and gave me the whole history of my life; he told me of a lover I had in this country, and described Worthy exactly, but in nothing so well as in his present indifference – I fled to him for refuge here today – he never so much as encouraged me in my fright, but coldly told me that he was sorry for the accident, because it might give the town cause to censure my conduct; excused his not waiting on me home, made a careless bow, and walked off. 'Sdeath, I could have stabbed him, or myself, 'twas the same thing. – Yonder he comes – I will so slave him.

LUCY

Don't exasperate him, consider what the fortune-teller told you; men are scarce, and as times go, it is not impossible for a woman to die a maid.

Enter WORTHY

MELINDA

No matter.

WORTHY

I find she's warmed, I must strike while the iron is hot. – You have a great deal of courage, madam, to venture into the walks where you were so late frighted.

MELINDA

And you have a quantity of impudence to appear before me, that you have so lately affronted.

WORTHY

I had no design to affront you, nor appear before you either, madam; I left you here because I had business in another place, and came hither thinking to meet another person.

MELINDA

Since you find yourself disappointed, I hope you'll withdraw to another part of the walk.

WORTHY

The walk is broad enough for us both. (*They walk by one another, he with his hat cocked, she fretting and tearing her fan*) Will you please to take snuff, madam?

He offers her his box, she strikes it out of his hand; while he is gathering it up,

Enter BRAZEN

BRAZEN

What, here before me, my dear!

Takes MELINDA *round the waist*

MELINDA

What means this insolence? *She cuffs him*

LUCY

(*To* BRAZEN) Are you mad? Don't you see Mr Worthy?

BRAZEN

No, no, I'm struck blind – Worthy! – Adso, well turned, my mistress has wit at her fingers' ends – madam, I ask your pardon, 'tis our way abroad – Mr Worthy, you're the happy man.

WORTHY

I don't envy your happiness very much, if the lady can afford no other sort of favours but what she has bestowed upon you.

MELINDA

I'm sorry the favour miscarried, for it was designed for you, Mr Worthy; and be assured, 'tis the last and only favour you must expect at my hands. – Captain, I ask your pardon.

Exit with LUCY

BRAZEN

I grant it. – You see, Mr Worthy, 'twas only a random shot, it might ha' taken off your head as well as mine; courage, my dear, 'tis the fortune of war; but the enemy has thought fit to withdraw, I think.

WORTHY

Withdraw! Oons, sir, what d'ye mean by withdraw?

BRAZEN
I'll show you. *Exit*

WORTHY
She's lost, irrecoverably lost, and Plume's advice has ruined me; 'sdeath, why should I that knew her haughty spirit be ruled by a man that's a stranger to her pride.

Enter PLUME

PLUME
Ha, ha, ha, a battle royal; don't frown so, man, she's your own, I tell'ee; I saw the fury of her love in the extremity of her passion, the wildness of her anger is a certain sign that she loves you to madness. That rogue, Kite, began the battle with abundance of conduct, and will bring you off victorious, my life on't; he plays his part admirably; she's to be with him again presently.

WORTHY
But what could be the meaning of Brazen's familiarity with her?

PLUME
You are no logician if you pretend to draw consequences from the actions of fools; there's no arguing by the rule of reason upon a science without principles, and such is their conduct; whim, unaccountable whim, hurries 'em on, like a man drunk with brandy before ten o'clock in the morning – but we lose our sport; Kite has opened above an hour ago, let's away. *Exeunt*

[Act IV], Scene ii

A Chamber

KITE, *disguised in a strange habit, sitting at a table,* [*whereon are books and globes;* SERVANT *in attendance*]

KITE (*Rising*)
By the position of the heavens, gained from my observation upon these celestial globes, I find that Luna was a tide-waiter, Sol a surveyor, Mercury a thief, Venus a whore, Saturn an alderman, Jupiter a rake, and Mars a sergeant of grenadiers; and this is the system of Kite the conjurer.

Enter PLUME *and* WORTHY

PLUME
Well, what success?

KITE

I have sent away a shoemaker and a tailor already, one's to be a captain of marines and the other a major of dragoons, I am to manage them at night. Have you seen the lady, Mr Worthy?

WORTHY

Aye, but it won't do – have you showed her her name that I tore off from the bottom of the letter?

KITE

No, sir, I reserve that for the last stroke.

PLUME

What letter?

WORTHY

One that I would not let you see, for fear you should break windows in good earnest. *Knocking at the door*

KITE

Officers to your post. *Exeunt* WORTHY *and* PLUME
Tycho, mind the door.

SERVANT *opens the door, enter* [THOMAS,] *a* SMITH

SMITH

Well, master, are you the cunning man?

KITE

I am the learned Copernicus.

SMITH

Well, Master Coppernose, I'm but a poor man and I can't afford above a shilling for my fortune.

KITE

Perhaps that is more than 'tis worth.

SMITH

Look'ee, doctor, let me have something that's good for my shilling, or I'll have my money again.

KITE

If there be faith in the stars, you shall have your shilling forty fold. Your hand, countryman – you are by trade a smith.

SMITH

How the devil should you know that?

KITE

Because the devil and you are brother tradesmen – you were born under Forceps.

SMITH

Forceps, what's that?

KITE

One of the signs; there's Leo, Sagittarius, Forceps, Furnes,

Dixmude, Namur, Brussels, Charleroi, and so forth – twelve of 'em. Let me see – did you ever make any bombs or cannon-bullets?

SMITH

Not I.

KITE

You either have, or will – the stars have decreed that you shall be – I must have more money, sir, your fortune's great –

SMITH

Faith, doctor, I have no more.

KITE

Oh, sir, I'll trust you, and take it out of your arrears.

SMITH

Arrears! What arrears?

KITE

The five hundred pound that's owing to you from the government.

SMITH

Owing me!

KITE

Owing you, sir – let me see your t'other hand – I beg your pardon, it will be owing to you; and the rogue of an agent will demand fifty per cent for a fortnight's advance.

SMITH

I'm in the clouds, doctor, all this while.

KITE

Sir, I am above 'em, among the stars – in two years, three months, and two hours, you will be made Captain of the Forges to the Grand Train of Artillery, and will have ten shillings a day and two servants; 'tis the decree of the stars, and of the fixed stars, that are as immovable as your anvil. Strike, sir, while the iron is hot – fly, sir, begone –

SMITH

What! What would you have me do, doctor? I wish the stars would put me in a way for this fine place.

KITE

The stars do – let me see – aye, about an hour hence walk carelessly into the market-place and you'll see a tall, slender gentleman cheapening a pen'worth of apples, with a cane hanging upon his button – this gentleman will ask you what's o'clock – he's your man, and the maker of your fortune; follow him, follow him. And now go home and take leave of your wife and children; an hour hence exactly is your time.

SMITH
A tall, slender gentleman, you say! With a cane. Pray, what sort of a head has the cane?

KITE
An amber head with a black ribband.

SMITH
But pray, of what employment is the gentleman?

KITE
Let me see – he's either a collector of the excise, or a plenipotentiary, or a captain of grenadiers – I can't tell exactly which. But he'll call you honest – your name is –

SMITH
Thomas.

KITE
He'll call you honest Tom.

SMITH
But how the devil should he know my name?

KITE
Oh, there are several sorts of Toms – Tom a'Lincoln, Tomtit, Tom Telltroth, Tom o'Bedlam, Tom Fool. – (*Knocking at the door*) Begone – an hour hence precisely.

SMITH
You say he'll ask me what's o'clock?

KITE
Most certainly, and you'll answer you don't know, and be sure you look at St Mary's dial, for the sun won't shine, and if it should, you won't be able to tell the figures.

SMITH
I will, I will. *Exit*

PLUME ([*Appearing*] *behind*)
Well done, conjurer, go on and prosper.

KITE
As you were.

Enter [PLUCK] *a* BUTCHER

KITE (*Aside*)
What, my old friend Pluck the butcher – I offered the surly bulldog five guineas this morning and he refused it.

BUTCHER
So, Master Conjurer, here's half a crown – and now you must understand –

KITE
Hold, friend, I know your business beforehand.

BUTCHER

You're devilish cunning then; for I don't well know it myself.

KITE

I know more than you, friend – you have a foolish saying, that such a one knows no more than the man in the moon; I tell you the man in the moon knows more than all the men under the sun; don't the moon see all the world?

BUTCHER

All the world see the moon, I must confess.

KITE

Then she must see all the world, that's certain. Give me your hand – you're by trade either a butcher or a surgeon.

BUTCHER

True, I am a butcher.

KITE

And a surgeon you will be, the employments differ only in the name – he that can cut up an ox, may dissect a man, and the same dexterity that cracks a marrow-bone will cut off a leg or an arm.

BUTCHER

What d'ye mean, doctor, what d'ye mean?

KITE

Patience, patience, Mr Surgeon-General, the stars are great bodies and move slowly.

BUTCHER

But what d'ye mean by Surgeon-General, doctor?

KITE

Nay, sir, if your worship won't have patience, I must beg the favour of your worship's absence.

BUTCHER

My worship, my worship! But why my worship?

KITE

Nay, then I have done. *Sits*

BUTCHER

Pray, doctor.

KITE

Fire and fury, sir! (*Rises in a passion*) Do you think the stars will be hurried? Do the stars owe you any money, sir, that you dare to dun their lordships at this rate? Sir, I am porter to the stars, and I am ordered to let no dun come near their doors.

BUTCHER

Dear doctor, I never had any dealings with the stars, they don't owe me a penny – but since you are their porter, please to accept of this half-crown to drink their healths, and don't be angry.

KITE

Let me see your hand then once more – here has been gold – five guineas, my friend, in this very hand this morning.

BUTCHER

Nay, then he is the devil – pray, doctor, were you born of a woman, or did you come into the world of your own head?

KITE

That's a secret – this gold was offered you by a proper, handsome man, called Hawk, or Buzzard, or –

BUTCHER

Kite, you mean.

KITE

Aye, aye, Kite.

BUTCHER

As errant a rogue as ever carried a halberd – the impudent rascal would have decoyed me for a soldier.

KITE

A soldier! A man of your substance for a soldier! Your mother has a hundred pound in hard money lying at this minute in the hands of a mercer, not forty yards from this place.

BUTCHER

Oons, and so she has, but very few know so much.

KITE

I know it, and that rogue, what's his name, Kite, knew it, and offered you five guineas to list because he knew your poor mother would give the hundred for your discharge.

BUTCHER

There's a dog now – flesh, doctor, I'll give you t'other half-crown, and tell me that this same Kite will be hanged.

KITE

He's in as much danger as any man in the county of Salop.

BUTCHER

There's your fee – but you have forgot the Surgeon-General all this while.

KITE

You put the stars in a passion. *Looks on his books*
But now they're pacified again – let me see – did you never cut off a man's leg?

BUTCHER

No.

KITE

Recollect, pray.

BUTCHER

I say no.

KITE

That's strange, wonderful strange; but nothing is strange to me, such wonderful changes have I seen – the second or third, aye, the third campaign that you make in Flanders, the leg of a great officer will be shattered by a great shot; you will be there accidentally, and with your cleaver chop off the limb at a blow; in short, the operation will be performed with so much dexterity, that with general applause you will be made Surgeon-General of the whole army.

BUTCHER

Nay, for the matter of cutting off a limb, I'll do't, I'll do't with any surgeon in Europe, but I have no thoughts of making a campaign.

KITE

You have no thoughts! What matter for your thoughts? The stars have decreed it, and you must go.

BUTCHER

The stars decree it! Oons, sir, the justices can't press me.

KITE

Nay, friend, 'tis none of my business, I ha' done. Only mind this, you'll know more an hour and a half hence – that's all – farewell. *Going*

BUTCHER

Hold, hold, doctor, Surgeon-General! What is the place worth, pray?

KITE

Five hundred pound a year, beside guineas for claps.

BUTCHER

Five hundred pound a year! – An hour and half hence you say?

KITE

Prithee, friend, be quiet, don't be so troublesome, here's such a work to make a booby butcher accept five hundred pound a year. – But if you must hear it – I tell you in short, you'll be standing in your stall an hour and half hence, and a gentleman will come by with a snuff-box in his hand, and the tip of his handkerchief hanging out of his right pocket; he'll ask you the price of a loin of veal, and at the same time stroke your great dog upon the head and call him Chopper.

BUTCHER
Mercy upon us! Chopper is the dog's name.

KITE
Look'ee there – what I say is true, things that are to come must come to pass. Get you home, sell off your stock, don't mind the whining and the snivelling of your mother and your sister, women always hinder preferment; make what money you can and follow that gentleman, his name begins with a P – mind that. There will be the barber's daughter, too, that you promised marriage to, she will be pulling and hauling you to pieces.

BUTCHER
What! Know Sally too? He's the devil, and he needs must go that the devil drives. – (*Going*) The tip of his handkerchief out of his left pocket?

KITE
No, no, his right pocket; if it be the left, 'tis none of the man.

BUTCHER
Well, well, I'll mind him. *Exit*

PLUME (*Behind with his pocket-book*)
The right pocket, you say?

KITE
I hear the rustling of silks. (*Knocking*) Fly, sir, 'tis Madam Melinda.

Enter MELINDA *and* LUCY

KITE [*To* SERVANT]
Tycho, chairs for the ladies.

MELINDA
Don't trouble yourself, we shan't stay, doctor.

KITE
Your ladyship is to stay much longer than you imagine.

MELINDA
For what?

KITE
For a husband. – (*To* LUCY) For your part, madam, you won't stay for a husband.

LUCY
Pray, doctor, do you converse with the stars, or with the devil?

KITE
With both; when I have the destinies of men in search, I consult the stars; when the affairs of women come under my

hand, I advise with my t'other friend.

MELINDA

And have you raised the devil upon my account?

KITE

Yes, madam, and he's now under the table.

LUCY

Oh, heavens protect us! Dear madam, let us be gone.

KITE

If you be afraid of him, why do you come to consult him? 210

MELINDA

Don't fear, fool. Do you think, sir, that because I'm a woman I'm to be fooled out of my reason, or frighted out of my senses? – Come, show me this devil.

KITE

He's a little busy at present, but when he has done he shall wait on you. 215

MELINDA

What is he doing?

KITE

Writing your name in his pocket-book.

MELINDA

Ha, ha, ha, my name! Pray, what have you or he to do with my name?

KITE

Look'ee, fair lady – the devil is a very modest person, he seeks 220 nobody unless they seek him first; he's chained up like a mastiff, and can't stir unless he be let loose. – You come to me to have your fortune told – do you think, madam, that I can answer you of my own head? No, madam, the affairs of women are so irregular, that nothing less than the devil can 225 give any account of 'em. Now to convince you of your incredulity, I'll show you a trial of my skill. – Here, you *Cacodemo del Plumo*, exert your power, – draw me this lady's name, the word Melinda, in the proper letters and character of her own handwriting. – Do it at three motions – one – 230 two – three – 'tis done – now, madam, will you please to send your maid to fetch it.

LUCY

I fetch it! The devil fetch me if I do.

MELINDA

My name in my own handwriting! That would be convincing indeed. 235

KITE

Seeing's believing. *Goes to the table, lifts up the carpet* Here Tre, Tre, poor Tre, give me the bone, sirrah. – There's your name upon that square piece of paper – behold –

MELINDA

'Tis wonderful! My very letters to a tittle.

LUCY

'Tis like your hand, madam, but not so like your hand neither, and now I look nearer, 'tis not like your hand at all.

KITE

Here's a chambermaid now will out-lie the devil.

LUCY

Look'ee, madam, they shan't impose upon us; people can't remember their hands no more than they can their faces. – Come, madam, let us be certain, write your name upon this paper, then we'll compare the two names.

Takes out paper and folds it

KITE

Anything for your satisfaction, madam – here's pen and ink.

MELINDA *writes*, LUCY *holds the paper*

LUCY

Let me see it, madam, 'tis the same, the very same. – (*Aside*) But I'll secure one copy for my own affairs.

MELINDA

This is demonstration.

KITE

'Tis so, madam, the word 'demonstration' comes from Dacmon the father of lies.

MELINDA

Well, doctor, I'm convinced; and now pray what account can you give me of my future fortune?

KITE

Before the sun has made one course round this earthly globe, your fortune will be fixed for happiness or misery.

MELINDA

What! So near the crisis of my fate!

KITE

Let me see – about the hour of ten tomorrow morning you will be saluted by a gentleman who will come to take his leave of you, being designed for travel. His intention of going abroad is sudden, and the occasion a woman. Your fortune and his are like the bullet and the barrel, one runs plump into the t'other. – In short, if the gentleman travels he will die abroad, and if he does you will die before he comes home.

MELINDA
What sort of man is he?

KITE
Madam, he's a fine gentleman, and a lover – that is, a man of very good sense, and a very great fool.

MELINDA
How is that possible, doctor?

KITE
Because, madam – because it is so: a woman's reason is the best for a man's being a fool.

MELINDA
Ten o'clock, you say?

KITE
Ten, about the hour of tea-drinking throughout the kingdom.

MELINDA
Here, doctor. (*Gives money*) Lucy, have you any questions to ask?

LUCY
Oh, madam! a thousand.

KITE
I must beg your patience till another time, for I expect more company this minute; besides, I must discharge the gentleman under the table.

LUCY
Oh, pray, sir, discharge us first.

KITE
Tycho, wait on the ladies downstairs.

Exit MELINDA *and* LUCY

Enter PLUME *and* WORTHY

KITE
Mr Worthy, you were pleased to wish me joy today, I hope to be able to return the compliment tomorrow.

WORTHY
I'll make it the best compliment to you that ever I made in my life, if you do; but I must be a traveller, you say?

KITE
No farther than the chops of the Channel, I presume, sir.

PLUME
That we have concerted already. (*Knocking hard*) Hey day! You don't profess midwifery, doctor?

KITE
Away to your ambuscade. *Exeunt* PLUME *and* WORTHY

Enter BRAZEN

BRAZEN
Your servant, servant, my dear.

KITE
Stand off, I have my familiar already.

BRAZEN
Are you bewitched, my dear?

KITE
Yes, my dear, but mine is a peaceable spirit, and hates gunpowder – thus I fortify myself; (*draws a circle round him*) and now, Captain, have a care how you force my lines.

BRAZEN
Lines! What dost talk of lines? You have something like a fishing-rod there, indeed; but I come to be acquainted with you, man – what's your name, my dear?

KITE
Conundrum.

BRAZEN
Conundrum! Rat me, I know a famous doctor in London of your name – where were you born?

KITE
I was born in Algebra.

BRAZEN
Algebra! – 'Tis no country in Christendom I'm sure, unless it be some pitiful place in the Highlands of Scotland.

KITE
Right! I told you I was bewitched.

BRAZEN
So am I, my dear, I'm going to be married – I've had two letters from a lady of fortune that loves me to madness, fits, colic, spleen, and vapours – shall I marry her in four and twenty hours, aye or no?

KITE
I must have the year and day o'th' month when these letters were dated.

BRAZEN
Why, you old bitch, did you ever hear of love-letters dated with the year and day o'th' month? Do you think *billets doux* are like bank bills?

KITE
They are not so good – but if they bear no date, I must examine the contents.

BRAZEN

Contents, that you shall, old boy, [*pulls out two letters*] here they be both.

KITE

Only the last you received, if you please. (*Takes the letter*) Now, sir, if you please to let me consult my books for a minute, I'll send this letter enclosed to you with the determination of the stars upon it to your lodgings.

BRAZEN

With all my heart – I must give him – (*puts his hand in his pocket*) Algebra! I fancy, doctor, 'tis hard to calculate the place of your nativity – here. – (*Gives him money*) And if I succeed, I'll build a watchtower upon the top of the highest mountain in Wales for the study of astrology, and the benefit of Conundrums. *Exit*

Enter PLUME *and* WORTHY

WORTHY

Oh! Doctor, that letter's worth a million, let me see it – and now I have it, I'm afraid to open it.

PLUME

Pho, let me see it! (*Opening the letter*) If she be a jilt – damn her, she is one – there's her name at the bottom on't.

WORTHY

How! – Then I'll travel in good earnest – by all my hopes, 'tis Lucy's hand.

PLUME

Lucy's!

WORTHY

Certainly, 'tis no more like Melinda's character than black is to white.

PLUME

Then 'tis certainly Lucy's contrivance to draw in Brazen for a husband – but are you sure 'tis not Melinda's hand?

WORTHY

You shall see; where's the bit of paper I gave you just now that the devil writ 'Melinda' upon?

KITE

Here, sir.

PLUME

'Tis plain, they're not the same; and is this the malicious name that was subscribed to the letter which made Mr Balance send his daughter into the country?

WORTHY

The very same, the other fragments I showed you just now. 345

PLUME

But 'twas barbarous to conceal this so long, and to continue me so many hours in the pernicious heresy of believing that angelic creature could change – poor Silvia!

WORTHY

Rich Silvia, you mean, and poor captain – ha, ha, ha; come, come, friend, Melinda is true and shall be mine; Silvia is 350 constant and may be yours.

PLUME

No, she's above my hopes – but for her sake I'll recant my opinion of her sex.

By some the sex is blamed without design,
Light, harmless censure, such as yours and mine, 355
Sallies of wit, and vapours of our wine.
Others the justice of the sex condemn,
And wanting merit to create esteem,
Would hide their own defects by censuring them.
But they, secure in their all-conqu'ring charms, 360
Laugh at the vain efforts of false alarms;
He magnifies their conquests who complains,
For none would struggle were they not in chains.

Exeunt

Act V, Scene i

An Antechamber [*adjoining* SILVIA'*s bedroom*], *with a periwig, hat, and sword upon the table*
Enter SILVIA *in her nightcap*

SILVIA

I have rested but indifferently, and I believe my bedfellow was as little pleased; poor Rose! Here she comes –

Enter ROSE

Good morrow, my dear, how d'ye this morning?

ROSE

Just as I was last night, neither better nor worse for you.

SILVIA

What's the matter? Did you not like your bedfellow? 5

ROSE

I don't know whether I had a bedfellow or not.

SILVIA
Did not I lie with you?

ROSE
No – I wonder you could have the conscience to ruin a poor girl for nothing.

SILVIA
I have saved thee from ruin, child; don't be melancholy, I can give you as many fine things as the captain can.

ROSE
But you can't, I'm sure. *Knocking at the door*

SILVIA
Odso! My accoutrements – (*Puts on her periwig, hat, and sword*) Who's at the door?

[CONSTABLE (*without*)]
Open the door, or we'll break it down.

SILVIA
Patience a little – *Opens the door*

Enter [MR BRIDEWELL, *a*] CONSTABLE *and* WATCH

CONSTABLE
We have 'em, we have 'em, the duck and the mallard both in the decoy.

SILVIA
What means this riot? Stand off! (*Draws*) The man dies that comes within reach of my point.

CONSTABLE
That is not the point, master, put up your sword or I shall knock you down; and so I command the Queen's peace.

SILVIA
You are some blockhead of a constable.

CONSTABLE
I am so, and have a warrant to apprehend the bodies of you and your whore there.

ROSE
Whore! Never was poor woman so abused.

Enter BULLOCK *unbuttoned*

BULLOCK
What's matter now? – Oh! Mr Bridewell, what brings you abroad so early?

CONSTABLE
This, sir – (*Lays hold of* BULLOCK) You're the Queen's prisoner.

BULLOCK

Wauns, you lie, sir, I'm the Queen's soldier.

CONSTABLE

No matter for that, you shall go before Justice Balance.

SILVIA

Balance! 'Tis what I wanted. – Here, Mr Constable, I resign my sword.

ROSE

Can't you carry us before the captain, Mr Bridewell?

CONSTABLE

Captain! Han't you got your bellyful of captains yet? Come, come, make way there. *Exeunt*

[Act V], Scene ii

JUSTICE BALANCE'*s house*
Enter BALANCE *and* SCALE

SCALE

I say 'tis not to be borne, Mr Balance.

BALANCE

Look'ee, Mr Scale, for my own part I shall be very tender in what regards the officers of the army; they expose their lives to so many dangers for us abroad that we may give them some grains of allowance at home.

SCALE

Allowance! This poor girl's father is my tenant, and if I mistake not, her mother nursed a child for you; shall they debauch our daughters to our faces?

BALANCE

Consider, Mr Scale, that were it not for the bravery of these officers we should have French dragoons among us, that would leave us neither liberty, property, wife, nor daughter. – Come, Mr Scale, the gentlemen are vigorous and warm, and may they continue so; the same heat that stirs them up to love, spurs them on to battle; you never knew a great general in your life that did not love a whore. This I only speak in reference to Captain Plume, for the other spark I know nothing of.

SCALE

Nor can I hear of anybody that does – oh, here they come.

Enter SILVIA, BULLOCK, ROSE, *prisoners*; CONSTABLE *and* WATCH

CONSTABLE

May it please your worships, we took them in the very act, *re infecta*, sir – the gentleman indeed behaved himself like a gentleman, for he drew his sword and swore, and afterwards laid it down and said nothing.

BALANCE

Give the gentleman his sword again – wait you without.

Exeunt CONSTABLE *and* WATCH

(*To* SILVIA) I'm sorry, sir, to know a gentleman upon such terms, that the occasion of our meeting should prevent the satisfaction of an acquaintance.

SILVIA

Sir, you need make no apology for your warrant, no more than I shall do for my behaviour – my innocence is upon an equal foot with your authority.

SCALE

Innocence! Have you not seduced that young maid?

SILVIA

No, Mr Goosecap, she seduced me.

BULLOCK

So she did, I'll swear – for she proposed marriage first.

BALANCE

What! Then you're married, child? (*To* ROSE)

ROSE

Yes, sir, to my sorrow.

BALANCE

Who was witness?

BULLOCK

That was I – I danced, threw the stocking, and spoke jokes by their bedside, I'm sure.

BALANCE

Who was the minister?

BULLOCK

Minister! We are soldiers, and want no ministers – they were married by the Articles of War.

BALANCE

Hold thy prating, fool. Your appearance, sir, promises some understanding; pray, what does this fellow mean?

SILVIA

He means marriage, I think – but that, you know, is so odd a thing, that hardly any two people under the sun agree in the ceremony; some make it a sacrament, others a convenience, and others make it a jest; but among soldiers 'tis most sacred – our sword, you know, is our honour; that we lay down, the hero jumps over it first, and the amazon after – leap rogue, follow whore – the drum beats a ruff, and so to bed; that's all, the ceremony is concise.

BULLOCK

And the prettiest ceremony, so full of pastime and prodigality –

BALANCE

What! Are you a soldier?

BULLOCK

Aye, that I am. Will your worship lend me your cane, and I'll show you how I can exercise.

BALANCE

Take it. (*Strikes him over the head*) Pray, sir, what commission may you bear? (*To* SILVIA)

SILVIA

I'm called Captain, sir, by all the coffeemen, drawers, whores, and groom-porters in London, for I wear a red coat, a sword, a hat *bien troussé*, a martial twist in my cravat, a fierce knot in my periwig, a cane upon my button, piquet in my head, and dice in my pocket.

SCALE

Your name, pray, sir?

SILVIA

Captain Pinch; I cock my hat with a pinch, I take snuff with a pinch, pay my whores with a pinch; in short, I can do anything at a pinch, but fight and fill my belly.

BALANCE

And pray, sir, what brought you into Shropshire?

SILVIA

A pinch, sir: I knew you country gentlemen want wit, and you know that we town gentlemen want money, and so –

BALANCE

I understand you, sir. – Here, Constable!

Enter CONSTABLE

Take this gentleman into custody till farther orders.

ROSE

Pray your worship, don't be uncivil to him, for he did me no hurt; he's the most harmless man in the world, for all he talks so.

SCALE

Come, come, child, I'll take care of you.

SILVIA

What, gentlemen, rob me of my freedom and my wife at

once! 'Tis the first time they ever went together.

BALANCE (*Whispers*)

Hark'ee, Constable –

CONSTABLE

It shall be done, sir. – Come along, sir.

Exeunt CONSTABLE, BULLOCK, [ROSE] *and* SILVIA

BALANCE

Come, Mr Scale, we'll manage the spark presently. 80

Exeunt BALANCE *and* SCALE

[Act V], Scene iii

MELINDA'*s Apartment*

Enter MELINDA *and* WORTHY

MELINDA

(*Aside*) So far the prediction is right, 'tis ten exactly. – And pray sir, how long have you been in this travelling humour?

WORTHY

'Tis natural, madam, for us to avoid what disturbs our quiet.

MELINDA

Rather the love of change, which is more natural, may be the 5 occasion of it.

WORTHY

To be sure, madam, there must be charms in variety, else neither you nor I should be so fond of it.

MELINDA

You mistake, Mr Worthy, I am not so fond of variety as to travel for't, nor do I think it prudence in you to run your- 10 self into a certain expense and danger, in hopes of precarious pleasures which at best never answer expectation, as 'tis evident from the example of most travellers, that long more to return to their own country than they did to go abroad. 15

WORTHY

What pleasures I may receive abroad are indeed uncertain; but this I am sure of, I shall meet with less cruelty among the most barbarous nations than I have found at home.

MELINDA

Come, sir, you and I have been jangling a great while; I fancy if we made up our accounts, we should the sooner 20 come to an agreement.

WORTHY

Sure, madam, you won't dispute your being in my debt –

my fears, sighs, vows, promises, assiduities, anxieties, jealousies, have run on for a whole year, without any payment.

MELINDA

A year! Oh Mr Worthy, what you owe to me is not to be paid under a seven years' servitude. How did you use me the year before, when taking the advantage of my innocence and necessity, you would have made me your mistress, that is, your slave? Remember the wicked insinuations, artful baits, deceitful arguments, cunning pretences; then your impudent behaviour, loose expressions, familiar letters, rude visits; remember those, those, Mr Worthy.

WORTHY

(*Aside*) I do remember, and am sorry I made no better use of 'em. – But you may remember, madam, that –

MELINDA

Sir, I'll remember nothing – 'tis your interest that I should forget; you have been barbarous to me, I have been cruel to you; put that and that together, and let one balance the other. Now if you will begin upon a new score, lay aside your adventuring airs, and behave yourself handsomely till Lent be over, here's my hand, I'll use you as a gentleman should be.

WORTHY

And if I don't use you as a gentlewoman should be, may this be my poison. *Kissing her hand*

Enter SERVANT

SERVANT

Madam, the coach is at the door.

MELINDA

I'm going to Mr Balance's country-house to see my cousin Silvia; I have done her an injury, and can't be easy till I have asked her pardon.

WORTHY

I dare not hope for the honour of waiting on you.

MELINDA

My coach is full, but if you will be so gallant as to mount your own horses and follow us, we shall be glad to be overtaken; and if you bring Captain Plume with you, we shan't have the worse reception.

WORTHY

I'll endeavour it. *Exit* WORTHY *leading* MELINDA

[Act V], Scene iv

The Market-place

Enter PLUME *and* KITE

PLUME

A baker, a tailor, a smith, and a butcher – I believe the first colony planted at Virginia had not more trades in their company than I have in mine.

KITE

The butcher, sir, will have his hands full; for we have two sheep stealers among us – I hear of a fellow, too, committed just now for stealing of horses.

PLUME

We'll dispose of him among the dragoons. Have we ne'er a poulterer among us?

KITE

Yes, sir, the king of the gypsies is a very good one, he has an excellent hand at a goose or a turkey. Here's Captain Brazen, sir – I must go look after the men. *Exit*

Enter BRAZEN *reading a letter*

BRAZEN

Um, um, um, the canonical hour – um, um, very well. – My dear Plume! Give me a buss.

PLUME

Half a score if you will, my dear. [*They kiss*] What hast got in thy hand, child?

BRAZEN

'Tis a project for laying out a thousand pound.

PLUME

Were it not requisite to project first how to get it in?

BRAZEN

You can't imagine, my dear, that I want a thousand pound; I have spent twenty times as much in the service – now, my dear, pray advise me, my head runs much upon architecture; shall I build a privateer or a playhouse?

PLUME

An odd question – a privateer or a playhouse! 'Twill require some consideration. – Faith, I'm for a privateer.

BRAZEN

I'm not of your opinion, my dear – for in the first place a privateer may be ill-built.

PLUME
And so may a playhouse.
BRAZEN
But a privateer may be ill-manned.
PLUME
And so may a playhouse.
BRAZEN
But a privateer may run upon the shallows.
PLUME
Not so often as a playhouse. 30
BRAZEN
But, you know, a privateer may spring a leak.
PLUME
And I know that a playhouse may spring a great many.
BRAZEN
But suppose the privateer come home with a rich booty, we should never agree about our shares.
PLUME
'Tis just so in a playhouse – so by my advice, you shall fix 35 upon the privateer.
BRAZEN
Agreed – but if this twenty thousand should not be in specie –
PLUME
What twenty thousand?
BRAZEN
Hark'ee – *Whispers* 40
PLUME
Married!
BRAZEN
Presently, we're to meet about half a mile out of town at the waterside – and so forth – (*Reads*) 'For fear I should be known by any of Worthy's friends, you must give me leave to wear my mask till after the ceremony, which will make me 45 ever yours'. – Look'ee there, my dear dog –
Shows the bottom of the letter to PLUME
PLUME
Melinda! And by this light, her own hand! – Once more, if you please, my dear; her hand exactly! – Just now you say?
BRAZEN
This minute I must be gone.
PLUME
Have a little patience, and I'll go with you. 50

BRAZEN
No, no, I see a gentleman coming this way that may be inquisitive; 'tis Worthy, do you know him?

PLUME
By sight only.

BRAZEN
Have a care, the very eyes discover secrets – *Exit*

Enter WORTHY

WORTHY
To boot and saddle, Captain, you must mount. 55

PLUME
Whip and spur, Worthy, or you won't mount.

WORTHY
But I shall: Melinda and I are agreed; she's gone to visit Silvia, we are to mount and follow, and could we carry a parson with us, who knows what might be done for us both?

PLUME
Don't trouble your head, Melinda has secured a parson 60 already.

WORTHY
Already! Do you know more than I?

PLUME
Yes, I saw it under her hand – Brazen and she are to meet half a mile hence at the waterside, there to take boat, I suppose to be ferried over to the Elysian fields, if there be any 65 such thing in matrimony.

WORTHY
I parted with Melinda just now; she assured me she hated Brazen, and that she resolved to discard Lucy for daring to write letters to him in her name.

PLUME
Nay, nay, there's nothing of Lucy in this – I tell ye I saw 70 Melinda's hand as surely as this is mine.

WORTHY
But I tell you, she's gone this minute to Justice Balance's country-house.

PLUME
But I tell you, she's gone this minute to the waterside.

Enter a SERVANT

SERVANT (*to* WORTHY)
Madam Melinda has sent word that you need not trouble 75 yourself to follow her, because her journey to Justice

Balance's is put off, and she's gone to take the air another way.

WORTHY

How! Her journey put off?

PLUME

That is, her journey was a put-off to you.

WORTHY

'Tis plain, plain – but how, where, when is she to meet Brazen?

PLUME

Just now, I tell you, half a mile hence at the waterside.

WORTHY

Up, or down the water?

PLUME

That I don't know.

WORTHY

I'm glad my horses are ready. – Jack, get 'em out.

[*Exit* SERVANT]

PLUME

Shall I go with you?

WORTHY

Not an inch; I shall return presently.

PLUME

You'll find me at the hall; the justices are sitting by this time, and I must attend them. [*Exeunt severally*]

[Act V], Scene v

A Court of Justice

BALANCE, SCALE *and* SCRUPLE *upon the bench;*
CONSTABLE, KITE, *Mob* [*in attendance*]
KITE *and* CONSTABLE *advance forward*

KITE

Pray, who are those honourable gentlemen upon the bench?

CONSTABLE

He in the middle is Justice Balance, he on the right is Justice Scale, and he on the left is Justice Scruple, and I am Mr Constable, four very honest gentlemen.

KITE

Oh dear sir, I'm your most obedient servant. (*Saluting the* CONSTABLE) I fancy, sir, that your employment and mine are much the same, for my business is to keep people in order, and if they disobey, to knock 'em down; and then we're both staff-officers.

CONSTABLE

Nay, I'm a sergeant myself – of the militia. Come, brother, you shall see me exercise – suppose this a musket now. (*He puts his staff on his right shoulder*) Now I'm shouldered.

KITE

Aye, you're shouldered pretty well for a constable's staff, but for a musket you must put it on t'other shoulder, my dear.

CONSTABLE

Adso! That's true. – Come, now give the word o'command.

KITE

Silence.

CONSTABLE

Aye, aye, so we will, – we will be silent.

KITE

Silence, you dog, silence –

Strikes him over the head with his halberd

CONSTABLE

That's the way to silence a man with a witness! – What d'ye mean, friend?

KITE

Only to exercise you, sir.

CONSTABLE

Your exercise differs so from ours, that we shall ne'er agree about it; if my own captain had given me such a rap, I had taken the law of him.

Enter PLUME

BALANCE

Captain, you're welcome.

PLUME

Gentlemen, I thank'ee.

SCRUPLE

Come, honest Captain, sit by me. (PLUME *ascends, and sits upon the bench*) Now produce your prisoners – here, that fellow there – set him up. [CONSTABLE *brings first prisoner to the dock*] Mr Constable, what have you to say against this man?

CONSTABLE

I have nothing to say against him, an't please ye.

BALANCE

No? What made you bring him hither?

CONSTABLE

I don't know, an't please your worship.

SCRUPLE

Did not the contents of your warrant direct you what sort of men to take up?

CONSTABLE

I can't tell, an't please ye, I can't read.

SCRUPLE

A very pretty constable truly! I find we have no business here.

KITE

May it please the worshipful bench, I desire to be heard in this case, as being counsel for the Queen.

BALANCE

Come, Sergeant, you shall be heard, since nobody else will speak; we won't come here for nothing.

KITE

This man is but one man, the country may spare him and the army wants him; besides, he's cut out by nature for a grenadier: he's five foot ten inches high, he shall box, wrestle, or dance the Cheshire Round with any man in the county, he gets drunk every sabbath-day, and he beats his wife.

WIFE

You lie, sirrah, you lie, an't please your worship, he's the best-natured, pains-taking man in the parish, witness my five poor children.

SCRUPLE

A wife! And five children! You, Constable, you rogue, how durst you impress a man that has a wife and five children?

SCALE

Discharge him, discharge him.

BALANCE

Hold, gentlemen. – Hark'ee, friend, how do you maintain your wife and five children?

KITE

They live upon wild fowl and venison, sir; the husband keeps a gun, and kills all the hares and partridges within five mile round.

BALANCE

A gun! Nay, if he be so good at gunning he shall have enough on't – he may be of use against the French, for he shoots flying to be sure.

SCRUPLE

But his wife and children, Mr Balance!

WIFE

Aye, aye, that's the reason you would send him away: you know I have a child every year, and you're afraid they should come upon the parish at last.

PLUME

Look'ee there, gentlemen, the honest woman has spoke it at once; the parish had better maintain five children this year than six or seven the next; that fellow upon his high feeding may get you two or three beggars at a birth.

WIFE

Look'ee, Mr Captain, the parish shall get nothing by sending him away, for I won't lose my teeming-time if there be a man left in the parish.

BALANCE

Send that woman to the house of correction – and the man –

KITE

I'll take care o'him, if you please. *Takes him down*

SCALE

Here, you Constable, the next: set up that black-faced fellow, he has a gunpowder look; [CONSTABLE *sets up* SECOND PRISONER] what can you say against this man, Constable?

CONSTABLE

Nothing, but that he's a very honest man.

PLUME

Pray, gentlemen, let me have one honest man in my company for the novelty's sake.

BALANCE

What are you, friend?

SECOND PRISONER

A collier, I work in the coal-pits.

SCRUPLE

Look'ee, gentlemen, this fellow has a trade, and the Act of Parliament here expresses, that we are to impress no man that has any visible means of a livelihood.

KITE

May it please your worships, this man has no visible means of a livelihood, for he works underground.

PLUME

Well said, Kite – Besides, the army wants miners.

BALANCE

Right! And had we an order of government for't, we could raise you in this and the neighbouring county of Stafford five hundred colliers that would run you underground like moles, and do more service in a siege that all the miners in the army.

SCRUPLE

Well, friend, what have you to say for yourself?

SECOND PRISONER

I'm married.

KITE

Lack-a-day, so am I.

SECOND PRISONER

Here's my wife, poor woman.

BALANCE

Are you married, good woman?

WOMAN

I'm married in conscience.

KITE

May it please your worship, she's with child in conscience.

SCALE

Who married you, mistress?

WOMAN

My husband – we agreed that I should call him husband to avoid passing for a whore, and that he should call me wife to shun going for a soldier.

SCRUPLE

A very pretty couple! Pray, Captain, will you take 'em both?

PLUME

What say you, Mr Kite – will you take care of the woman?

KITE

Yes, sir, she shall go with us to the seaside and there if she has a mind to drown herself we'll take care that nobody shall hinder her. [*Takes down* SECOND PRISONER]

BALANCE

Here, Constable, bring in my man. *Exit* CONSTABLE

Now, Captain, I'll fit you with a man such as you ne'er listed in your life.

Enter CONSTABLE *and* SILVIA

Oh my friend Pinch, I'm very glad to see you.

SILVIA

Well, sir, and what then?

SCALE

What then! Is that your respect to the bench?

SILVIA

Sir, I don't care a farthing for you nor your bench neither.

SCRUPLE

Look'ee, gentlemen, that's enough, he's a very impudent fellow, and fit for a soldier.

SCALE

A notorious rogue, I say, and very fit for a soldier.

CONSTABLE

A whoremaster, I say, and therefore fit to go.

BALANCE

What think you, Captain?

PLUME

I think he's a very pretty fellow, and therefore fit to serve.

SILVIA

Me for a soldier! Send your own lazy, lubberly sons at home, fellows that hazard their necks every day in pursuit of a fox, yet dare not peep abroad to look an enemy in the face.

CONSTABLE

May it please your worships, I have a woman at the door to swear a rape against this rogue.

SILVIA

Is it your wife or daughter, booby? I ravished 'em both yesterday.

BALANCE

Pray, Captain, read the Articles of War, we'll see him listed immediately.

PLUME (*Reads*)

'Articles of War against Mutiny and Desertion . . .'

SILVIA

Hold, sir. – Once more, gentlemen, have a care what you do, for you shall severely smart for any violence you offer to me; and you, Mr Balance, I speak to you particularly, you shall heartily repent it.

PLUME

Look'ee, young spark, say but one word more and I'll build a horse for you as high as the ceiling, and make you ride the most tiresome journey that ever you made in your life.

SILVIA

You have made a fine speech, good Captain Huffcap, but you had better be quiet, I shall find a way to cool your courage.

PLUME

Pray, gentlemen, don't mind him, he's distracted.

SILVIA

'Tis false – I'm descended of as good a family as any in your county, my father is as good a man as any upon your bench, and I am heir to twelve hundred pound a year.

BALANCE

He's certainly mad – pray, Captain, read the Articles of War.

SILVIA

Hold, once more. – Pray, Mr Balance, to you I speak: suppose I were your child, would you use me at this rate?

BALANCE

No, faith, were you mine, I would send you to Bedlam first, and into the army afterwards.

SILVIA

But consider my father, sir, he's as good, as generous, as brave, as just a man as ever served his country; I'm his only child, perhaps the loss of me may break his heart.

BALANCE

He's a very great fool if it does. Captain, if you don't list him this minute I'll leave the court.

PLUME

Kite, do you distribute the levy-money to the men whilst I read.

KITE

Aye, sir, – silence, gentlemen.

PLUME *reads the Articles of War*

BALANCE

Very well; now, Captain, let me beg the favour of you not to discharge this fellow upon any account whatsoever. – Bring in the rest.

CONSTABLE

There are no more, an't please your worship.

BALANCE

No more! There were five two hours ago.

SILVIA

'Tis true, sir, but this rogue of a constable let the rest escape for a bribe of eleven shillings a man, because he said that the Act allows him but ten, so the odd shilling was clear gains.

ALL JUSTICES

How!

SILVIA

Gentlemen, he offered to let me get away for two guineas, but I had not so much about me. – This is truth, and I'm ready to swear it.

KITE

And I'll swear it, give me the book, 'tis for the good of the service.

SECOND PRISONER

May it please your worship, I gave him half a crown to say

that I was an honest man, – but now since that your worships have made me a rogue, I hope I shall have my money again.

BALANCE

'Tis my opinion that this constable be put into the captain's hands, and if his friends don't bring four good men for his ransom by tomorrow night – Captain, you shall carry him to Flanders.

SCALE, SCRUPLE

Agreed, agreed.

PLUME

Mr Kite, take the constable into custody.

KITE

Aye, aye, sir. – (*To the* CONSTABLE) Will you please to have your office taken from you, or will you handsomely lay down your staff as your betters have done before you?

The CONSTABLE *drops his staff*

BALANCE

Come, gentlemen, there needs no great ceremony in adjourning this court; – Captain, you shall dine with me.

KITE

Come Mr Militia Sergeant, I shall silence you now I believe, without your taking the law of me.

Exeunt omnes

[Act V], Scene vi

The Fields

Enter BRAZEN *leading in* LUCY *masked*

BRAZEN

The boat is just below here.

Enter WORTHY *with a case of pistols under his arm*

WORTHY

Here, sir, take your choice.

Going between 'em, and offering them

BRAZEN

What! Pistols! Are they charged, my dear?

WORTHY

With a brace of bullets each.

BRAZEN

But I'm a foot-officer, my dear, and never use pistols, the sword is my way – and I won't be put out of my road to please any man.

WORTHY

Nor I neither, so have at you. *Cocks one pistol*

BRAZEN

Look'ee, my dear, I don't care for pistols; – pray oblige me and let us have a bout at sharps; damn't there's no parrying these bullets.

WORTHY

Sir, if you han't your belly full of these, the swords shall come in for second course.

BRAZEN

Why then fire and fury! I have eaten smoke from the mouth of a cannon, sir, don't think I fear powder, for I live upon't. Let me see. (*Takes one*) And now, sir, how many paces distant shall we fire?

WORTHY

Fire you when you please, I'll reserve my shot till I be sure of you.

BRAZEN

Come, where's your cloak?

WORTHY

Cloak! What d'ye mean?

BRAZEN

To fight upon, I always fight upon a cloak, 'tis our way abroad.

LUCY

Come, gentlemen, I'll end the strife. *Unmasks*

WORTHY

Lucy! Take her.

BRAZEN

The devil take me if I do – Huzza! (*Fires his pistol*) D'ye hear, d'ye hear, you plaguey harridan, how those bullets whistle, suppose they had been lodged in my gizzard now? –

LUCY

Pray, sir, pardon me.

BRAZEN

I can't tell, child, till I know whether my money be safe. (*Searching his pockets*) Yes, yes, I do pardon you, – but if I had you in the Rose Tavern, Covent Garden, with three or four hearty rakes, and three or four smart napkins, I would tell you another story, my dear. *Exit*

WORTHY

And was Melinda privy to this?

LUCY

No, sir; she wrote her name upon a piece of paper at the fortune-teller's last night, which I put in my pocket, and so writ above it to the captain.

WORTHY

And how came Melinda's journey put off? 40

LUCY

At the town's end she met Mr Balance's steward, who told her that Mrs Silvia was gone from her father's, and nobody could tell whither.

WORTHY

Silvia gone from her father's! This will be news to Plume. Go home, and tell your lady how near I was being shot for 45 her. *Exeunt*

[Act V], Scene vii

[BALANCE's *house*]

Enter BALANCE *with a napkin in his hand, as risen from dinner, and* STEWARD

STEWARD

We did not miss her till the evening, sir, and then searching for her in the chamber that was my young master's, we found her clothes there, but the suit that your son left in the press when he went to London was gone.

BALANCE

The white, trimmed with silver! 5

STEWARD

The same.

BALANCE

You han't told that circumstance to anybody?

STEWARD

To none but your worship.

BALANCE

And be sure you don't. Go into the dining-room, and tell Captain Plume that I beg to speak with him. 10

STEWARD

I shall. *Exit*

BALANCE

Was ever man so imposed upon? I had her promise indeed that she should never dispose of herself without my consent. – I have consented with a witness, given her away as my act and deed – and this, I warrant, the captain thinks will pass; 15

no, I shall never pardon him the villainy, first of robbing me of my daughter, and then the mean opinion he must have of me to think that I could be so wretchedly imposed upon; her extravagant passion might encourage her in the attempt, but the contrivance must be his – I'll know the truth presently. 20

Enter PLUME

Pray, Captain, what have you done with your young gentleman soldier?

PLUME

He's at my quarters, I suppose, with the rest of my men.

BALANCE

Does he keep company with the common soldiers?

PLUME

No, he's generally with me. 25

BALANCE

He lies with you, I presume?

PLUME

No, faith, – I offered him part of my bed, but the young rogue fell in love with Rose, and has lain with her, I think, since he came to town.

BALANCE

So that between you both, Rose has been finely managed. 30

PLUME

Upon my honour, sir, she had no harm from me.

BALANCE

All's safe, I find. – Now, Captain, you must know that the young fellow's impudence in court was well grounded; he said I should heartily repent his being listed, and so I do from my soul. 35

PLUME

Aye! For what reason?

BALANCE

Because he is no less than what he said he was, born of as good a family as any in this county, and is heir to twelve hundred pound a year.

PLUME

I'm very glad to hear it, for I wanted but a man of that quality to make my company a perfect representative of the whole commons of England. 40

BALANCE

Won't you discharge him?

PLUME

Not under a hundred pound sterling.

BALANCE

You shall have it, for his father is my intimate friend.

PLUME

Then you shall have him for nothing.

BALANCE

Nay, sir, you shall have your price.

PLUME

Not a penny, sir; I value an obligation to you much above a hundred pound.

BALANCE

Perhaps, sir, you shan't repent your generosity. – Will you please to write his discharge in my pocket-book? (*Gives his book*) In the meantime we'll send for the gentleman. Who waits there?

Enter SERVANT

Go to the captain's lodgings and inquire for Mr Wilful; tell him his captain wants him here immediately.

SERVANT

Sir, the gentleman's below at the door inquiring for the captain.

PLUME

Bid him come up – here's the discharge, sir.

BALANCE

Sir, I thank you. – (*Aside*) 'Tis plain he had no hand in't.

Enter SILVIA

SILVIA

I think, Captain, you might have used me better, than to leave me yonder among your swearing, drunken crew; and you, Mr Justice, might have been so civil as to have invited me to dinner, for I have eaten with as good a man as your worship.

PLUME

Sir, you must charge our want of respect upon our ignorance of your quality – but now you're at liberty – I have discharged you.

SILVIA

Discharged me!

BALANCE

Yes, sir, and you must once more go home to your father.

SILVIA

My father! Then I'm discovered! Oh sir, (*kneeling*) I expect no pardon.

BALANCE

Pardon! No, no, child; your crime shall be your punishment; here, Captain, I deliver her over to the conjugal power for her chastisement; since she will be a wife, be you a husband, a very husband: when she tells you of her love, upbraid her with her folly; be modishly ungrateful, because she has been unfashionably kind; and use her worse than you would anybody else, because you can't use her so well as she deserves.

PLUME

And are you Silvia in good earnest?

SILVIA

Earnest! I have gone too far to make it a jest, sir.

PLUME

And do you give her to me in good earnest?

BALANCE

If you please to take her, sir.

PLUME

Why then I have saved my legs and arms, and lost my liberty; secure from wounds, I'm prepared for the gout; farewell subsistence and welcome taxes. – Sir, my liberty and hopes of being a general are much dearer to me than your twelve hundred pound a year – but to your love, madam, I resign my freedom, and to your beauty my ambition – greater in obeying at your feet, than commanding at the head of an army.

Enter WORTHY

WORTHY

I'm sorry to hear, Mr Balance, that your daughter is lost.

BALANCE

So am not I, sir, since an honest gentleman has found her.

Enter MELINDA

MELINDA

Pray, Mr Balance, what's become of my cousin Silvia?

BALANCE

Your cousin Silvia is talking yonder with your cousin Plume.

MELINDA
WORTHY

How!

SILVIA

Do you think it strange, cousin, that a woman should change? But, I hope, you'll excuse a change that has proceeded from constancy; I altered my outside because I was the same within, and only laid by the woman to make sure of my man; that's my history.

MELINDA

Your history is a little romantic, cousin, but since success has crowned your adventures you will have the world o' your side, and I shall be willing to go with the tide, provided you pardon an injury I offered you in the letter to your father.

PLUME

That injury, madam, was done to me, and the reparation I expect shall be made to my friend; make Mr Worthy happy, and I shall be satisfied.

MELINDA

A good example, sir, will go a great way – when my cousin is pleased to surrender, 'tis probable I shan't hold out much longer.

Enter BRAZEN

BRAZEN

Gentlemen, I am yours – madam, I am not yours.

MELINDA

I'm glad on't, sir.

BRAZEN

So am I. – You have got a pretty house here, Mr Laconic.

BALANCE

'Tis time to right all mistakes – my name, sir, is Balance.

BRAZEN

Balance! Sir, I'm your most obedient. – I know your whole generation – had not you an uncle that was governor of the Leeward Islands some years ago?

BALANCE

Did you know him?

BRAZEN

Intimately, sir – he played at billiards to a miracle; you had a brother, too, that was captain of a fireship – poor Dick – he had the most engaging way with him – of making punch, – and then his cabin was so neat – but his boy Jack was the most comical bastard – ha, ha, ha, ha, a pickled dog, I shall never forget him.

PLUME

Well, Captain, are you fixed in your project yet? Are you still for the privateer?

BRAZEN

No, no, I had enough of a privateer just now, I had like to have been picked up by a cruiser under false colours, and a French picaroon for aught I know.

PLUME
But have you got your recruits, my dear?
BRAZEN
Not a stick, my dear.
PLUME
Probably I shall furnish you.

Enter ROSE *and* BULLOCK

ROSE
Captain, Captain, I have got loose once more, and have persuaded my sweetheart Cartwheel to go with us, but you must promise not to part with me again.
SILVIA
I find Mrs Rose has not been pleased with her bedfellow.
ROSE
Bedfellow! I don't know whether I had a bedfellow or not.
SILVIA
Don't be in a passion, child, I was as little pleased with your company as you could be with mine.
BULLOCK
Pray, sir, dunna be offended at my sister, she's something underbred – but if you please I'll lie with you in her stead.
PLUME
I have promised, madam, to provide for this girl; now will you be pleased to let her wait upon you, or shall I take care of her?
SILVIA
She shall be my charge, sir, you may find it business enough to take care of me.
BULLOCK
Aye, and of me, Captain, for wauns! if ever you lift your hand against me, I'll desert.
PLUME
Captain Brazen shall take care o' that. – My dear, instead of the twenty thousand pound you talked of, you shall have the twenty brave recruits that I have raised, at the rate they cost me. – My commission I lay down to be taken up by some braver fellow, that has more merit and less good fortune, whilst I endeavour by the example of this worthy gentleman to serve my Queen and country at home.

With some regret I quit the active field,
Where glory full reward for life does yield;
But the recruiting trade, with all its train
Of lasting plague, fatigue, and endless pain,

I gladly quit, with my fair spouse to stay,
And raise recruits the matrimonial way.

Exeunt

EPILOGUE

All ladies and gentlemen that are willing to see the comedy called *The Recruiting Officer*, let them repair tomorrow night by six o'clock to the sign of the Theatre Royal in Drury Lane, and they shall be kindly entertained –

We scorn the vulgar ways to bid you come, 5
Whole Europe now obeys the call of drum.
The soldier, not the poet, here appears,
And beats up for a corps of volunteers;
He finds that music chiefly does delight ye,
And therefore chooses music to invite ye. 10

Beat the *Grenadier March* – Row, row, tow! – Gentlemen, this piece of music, called *An Overture to a Battle*, was composed by a famous Italian master, and was performed with wonderful success, at the great operas of Vigo, Schellenberg, and Blenheim; it came off with the applause of all Europe, 15 excepting France; the French found it a little too rough for their *delicatesse*.

Some that have acted on those glorious stages,
Are here to witness to succeeding ages
That no music like the *Grenadier's* engages. 20

Ladies, we must own that this music of ours is not altogether so soft as Bononcini's, yet we dare affirm, that it has laid more people asleep than all the *Camillas* in the world; and you'll condescend to own that it keeps one awake better than any opera that ever was acted. 25

The *Grenadier March* seems to be a composure excellently adapted to the genius of the English; for no music was ever followed so far by us, nor with so much alacrity; and with all deference to the present subscription, we must say that the *Grenadier March* has been subscribed for by the whole Grand 30 Alliance; and we presume to inform the ladies, that it always has the pre-eminence abroad, and is constantly heard by the tallest, handsomest men in the whole army. In short, to gratify the present taste, our author is now adapting some words to the *Grenadier March*, which he intends to have performed 35 tomorrow, if the lady who is to sing it should not happen to be sick.

This he concludes to be the surest way
To draw you hither, for you'll all obey
Soft music's call, though you should damn his play. 40